PROOF POSITIVE

by Walter Orechwa

© 2016 Walter Orechwa

All Rights Reserved.

No part of this publication may be reproduced, stored in a retrieval system, or transmitted, in any form or by any means, electronic, mechanical, photocopying, recording, or otherwise, without the written permission of the author.

First published by Dog Ear Publishing
4011 Vincennes Rd
Indianapolis, IN 46268
www.dogearpublishing.net

ISBN: 978-1-4575-5058-4

This book is printed on acid-free paper.

Printed in the United States of America

CONTENTS

Introduction: How to use this book 1

Chapter 1. A Short History of Organized Labor 5
    History of Unions: 1900–1950
    History of Unions: 1950–Today

Chapter 2. Why Become Union-Proof? 19
    The Cost of Unionization
    Job Security

Chapter 3. Organized Labor: An Inside Look 30
    The NLRB
    Union Corruption
    Union Finances
    Union Constitutions

Chapter 4. Union Organizing 55
    Four Paths to Representation
    Modern Labor Tactics
    Signs of an Organizing Campaign
    Representation: The Legal Process
    What Not to Say: T.I.P.S.
    What to Say: F.O.E.
    Labor Practice Charges

Chapter 5. Life with a Union 92
    Collective Bargaining
    Managing in a Union Environment
    The Truth About Strikes

Chapter 6. Getting Union-Proof 112
    Resources
    Vulnerability Assessment
    Employee Handbooks and Policies
    Getting Proactive - Preventive Measures
    Your Union-Free Philosophy
    Creating Your Union-Proof Culture

INTRODUCTION:

HOW TO USE THIS BOOK

Recently, we polled several thousand labor relations and human resources experts and asked them, "If you wanted to deliver the most essential training to your labor team to keep your company union-free, what *two* things would you communicate?"

The overwhelming majority of them said one of two things. The most common response was (no surprise) training supervisors and front-line managers. The second-most-common response? Well, that's something I'll share with you in just a moment. But first, when it comes to educating front-line managers, if your company is anything like mine, between the day-to-day operations of your company and the obligations you're already facing, I'm sure there just aren't enough hours in the day to properly educate your front-line managers.

As someone who's in charge of human resources and labor relations, and who is handling the responsibilities that come with being a CEO (and because my time is so limited!), I'm increasingly less likely to jump onto the next big thing. I imagine you, too, might be choosy about the business books in which you're willing to invest your time. But I also know that all it takes is just one pivotal idea for a book or resource to change your perspective on labor relations forever. I believe the book you now hold in your hands is one of those resources—truly worth the investment of your time. And not only that...

When you apply the concepts and knowledge found in *Proof Positive*, I honestly believe that it will deliver that second-most-common thing labor relations and human resources experts answered when asked to complete the sentence: "If I wanted to deliver training to keep my company union-free, I'd want to _____." What is that thing? How to build a genuinely union-proof culture, one that simply makes unions unnecessary. The reason I say that is because, as you're about to discover, the information in *Proof Positive* is responsible for creating union-proof companies across the country—inspiring workforces in industries ranging from aerospace to retail. And, in addition to the union-proofing effect these ideas are having in industry after industry, businesses using these ideas are becoming employers of choice—companies for which employees long to work! And even more importantly, by the time you finish this book, the *Proof Positive* concepts are something you'll be able to use in your business in a practical way. I want you to get the most out of this book in the least amount of time, so let me explain how I've organized *Proof Positive*.

This book is broken down into six main parts. Chapter 1 is devoted to understanding the history of organized labor. Then I will discuss the reasons for becoming union-proof. As I share with you some of the twists and turns of organized labor, we'll move on to an inside look at unions, including the NLRB, finances, and more. We continue with a journey into organizing and how unions do what they do. My hope is that these ideas will provide you with three things: first, a context for what union-proofing truly is; second, an understanding of the opportunities available to you to create a union-proof company; and third, and maybe most importantly, the inspiration to create a union-proof culture for your employees. The truth is nearly every company that has overcome an organizing attempt did so with the help of someone with knowledge and experience. I want that person to be you.

The final two chapters of this book will give you an idea of what it's like to manage a unionized workforce—and what it takes to become union-proof. Chapter 6 is the "methodology" section, which shows you what union-proofing is and how to implement it in your business in step-by-step detail. If you're the type of person who wants to skip the backstory and "cut to the chase," you can go straight to the Getting Union-Proof section in chapter 6. Of course, after reading it, if you want to go back and understand the foundation for these ideas, the entire approach will then make even more sense.

You are welcome to choose where to begin. That said, wherever you start (with the foundational material or with union-proofing), this book is intentionally designed to be interactive. What I mean by that is, by necessity, there is a blurring of offline and online worlds today. The days of a written book (or even an e-book) being nothing but a "book" are long gone. More often than not, these concepts are timeless, but with constant changes in labor laws and technology, their application can change rapidly. It is my goal to help you understand the concepts and strategies in *Proof Positive* as well as give you access to the most up-to-date application of those concepts.

You can get a sneak peek at how to union-proof your company by visiting: http://unionproof.com/certification. That being said, I want to point out something that will hopefully inspire you. I want you to understand: union-proofing is here in its entirety. I've held nothing back. It is all here for you to use and customize for your business. I've given you everything I can in the confines of one book so that you can use the ideas in *Proof Positive* successfully.

There you have it. The choice is yours. Start at the beginning or in the middle, whichever you prefer. But whatever you decide, the most important thing is simply to start. The UnionProof Team and I are committed to helping you create a union-proof culture and give you everything you need and more to take your business to the next level. So, without further delay, let's get started!

—Walter Orechwa
Chief Executive Officer
Projections, Inc.

CHAPTER 1

A Short History of Organized Labor

History of Unions: 1900–1950

Organized labor likes to use their "proud legacy" to market themselves. But the truth is, the romanticized history of unions is all but irrelevant in the twenty-first century. Instead of being the grassroots organizations they once were, unions have been fighting for survival for decades. That desperate struggle means they are now all about themselves—instead of being about the members—and that's why it's critical for your company to become union-proof.

The idea of workers coming together to solve issues is older than the United States itself. It seems like no sooner had colonists landed at Plymouth Rock than a historic labor event occurred, the Maine Indentured Servants' and Fisherman's Mutiny.

Back then, the movement was all about the independent American spirit—fighting for what was right—and a lot of the passion in the movement came in response to the demands placed on workers during the Industrial Revolution. Nineteenth-century working conditions were barely humane, the work was often dangerous, and employees weren't protected by laws or government agencies. Unions were needed to speak up for workers.

To gain more power and leverage, small craft unions gave way to the development of national labor associations like the

Knights of Labor, who fought for an eight-hour workday. By 1886, a whopping 20 percent of all workers were affiliated with the Knights of Labor, whose membership peaked at over 800,000 members. But all that influence and power came at a price: It didn't take long for these unions to begin fighting amongst themselves.

Their tightly knit ranks fractured to form the American Federation of Labor, a national alliance of craft unions who were unhappy with the Knights of Labor. Samuel Gompers was elected President of the newly formed AFL, and his leadership created a movement that grew more powerful...and more capable of taking on the pressing concerns of the day.

With the help of both craft and national unions, lawmakers in Washington began to recognize the plight of the American workers, and things began to change. In 1888, Congress created the Bureau of Labor, which eventually became today's U.S. Department of Labor.

The Machinists Union was founded in 1888, and the Mineworkers were next to organize in 1890, followed quickly by the Carpenters. Just two years later, dockworkers formed the Longshoremen's Union. The movement grew, and in 1899, drivers came together as the now-notorious Teamsters.

But along with the increase in union membership came an increase in worker strikes, including a notable strike in 1902 by anthracite coal miners. This UMW strike was the first work stoppage that required intervention by the federal government, and President Theodore Roosevelt intervened with the first-ever mediated agreement.

During World War I, that independent American spirit shone in a different way, as unions and companies worked together to achieve victory. Even as the war raged, unions worked to win important legal rights, including passage of the Adamson Act, establishing the eight-hour workday, with overtime, for railway workers.

But as productive as wartime had been, when World War I ended, the U.S. Labor Movement suddenly found itself at a critical crossroads. Americans were suddenly divided on the issue of support for labor unions, and those feelings came to a head during a series of nationwide strikes, starting with the Seattle General Strike.

For six days in 1919, Seattle, Washington, became the site of the very first "general strike" in American history. What had started as a simple shipyard workers' strike turned into chaos when thousands of other Seattle union workers joined them on the picket line, in an act of solidarity. The strike paralyzed the port city, and with the post–World War I "Red Scare" still in full effect, many condemned the union strike as a communist threat to American freedoms.

In the decade that followed, the labor movement had serious leadership shakeups. With post-wartime prosperity and a sharp decline in public opinion, unions were struggling to survive. But what Americans didn't know was that, like all good times, these, too, were about to come to an end. Just a few years before Black Tuesday, the Brotherhood of Sleeping Car Porters was established. The Brotherhood was the first labor organization led by African Americans to receive a charter in the AFL. Their founder and first president was A. Philip Randolph, who later became a leader in the civil rights movement.

As the country continued to suffer the effects of The Great Depression, unemployment rates reached 25 percent by the winter of 1932. Having so many workers unable to make a living hit the labor movement hard. Union membership numbers dropped, because workers simply couldn't afford to pay their dues, and funding numerous strikes against wage cuts had left unions impoverished. On top of these external challenges, unions continued to struggle internally with how they should be "organized" themselves.

Some believed a union should consist of workers who practiced a single, specific craft, while others felt they should include all employees in a single company or industry, regardless of the particular job. AFL leadership had long supported the tradition of craft unions, and they were reluctant to organize unskilled workers outside of a specific craft.

In 1935, United Mineworkers President John Lewis formed the "Congress of Industrial Organizations," within the AFL, to support industrial unions focused on a specific industry. The following year, the AFL expelled the members of the CIO, and in 1938 the CIO positioned themselves as a rival labor federation, creating two separate camps within the movement: the AFL and the CIO.

But while this internal debate was raging, public opinion about unions had shifted once again, presenting new opportunities for the labor movement. In the wake of a devastating Depression, many unemployed workers were left vulnerable, willing to listen to anyone offering any job security or protection—and political leaders soon followed the public's lead...

The Pullman Company was one of the largest single employers of African-Americans in the 1920s and 1930s. Like all companies, Pullman had its share of problems with employees—but the company stopped all union organizing efforts by the Brotherhood of Sleeping Car Porters by isolating or firing union leaders. Finally, the effort to organize Pullman by five hundred porters in Harlem led to a secret campaign, with Randolph chosen as the man to lead the effort. Randolph did not work for Pullman, and thus he was beyond retaliation by the company.

As a sign of the times, the Brotherhood of Sleeping Car Porters won the right to represent Pullman's porters and was certified on June 1, 1935, by the National Mediation Board under the Railway Labor Act.

In the 1930s, the government passed a series of legislative acts designed to support the efforts of organized labor and alleviate the economic crisis. The first of these acts outlawed agreements between employers and employees in which the employee agreed—as a condition of employment—not to join a labor union. These so-called "yellow dog contracts" were made illegal with the Norris–La Guardia Act, passed in 1932, which also prohibited federal intervention in labor disputes.

A year later, President Roosevelt tried to give workers government protections with the National Industrial Recovery Act. The Act contained minimum-wage and maximum-hour provisions, and it gave workers the right to organize into unions and enter collective bargaining.

In 1935, the Supreme Court said the Act was unconstitutional, but it was then replaced (just two months later) by the National Labor Relations Act, also known as the "Wagner Act." Congress enacted the NLRA to establish the right of all workers to organize and to elect representatives for collective bargaining purposes.

Roosevelt's National Industrial Recovery Act resurfaced in 1938, as the Fair Labor Standards Act. This act proposed government protections that included a forty-hour workweek, the idea of establishing a national minimum wage, guaranteeing time-and-a-half for certain work, and prohibiting most employment of minors.

With all of this labor-friendly legislation in place at the start of World War II, the stage was set for a dramatic upswing in union membership. In 1940, 18.3 percent of employed workers belonged to a union, but by the end of the war, just five years later, that percentage had surged to 27.1 percent, and it stayed at that level solidly through the rest of the 1940s.

But the war and postwar periods weren't all positive news for labor. Many unions chose to defy a wartime "no-strike" pledge, and millions of work hours were lost due to strikes at factories and in coal mines during the war. But that was nothing compared to what came in postwar America.

In 1946, "Great Strike Wave," a series of massive postwar labor strikes, took hold. The strikes spanned numerous industries and public utilities and involved five million workers. One strike in particular, by four hundred thousand mineworkers, in which government troops seized railroads and coal mines, had soured the public on strike actions.

Public perception was that large-scale strikes had damaged the U.S. economy. The combination of these strikes, along with their rise in political influence, and lingering Cold War hostilities, all contributed to growing anti-union sentiment after World War II. That independent American spirit that had served the unions so well was now turning against them, as Americans saw self-reliance as the path to a better future.

In response to the concern over strikes and the power of unions, the Taft-Hartley Act was passed in 1947, amending the National Labor Relations Act to restrict the activities and powers of labor unions. The Act added unfair labor practices for unions, prohibited closed shops, limited some kinds of strikes, pickets, and boycotts, and allowed states to adopt right-to-work laws.

Labor's rise in the first part of the twentieth century was hardly a smooth journey—rather, it was one filled with stops and starts and one that was both helped and hurt by the impact of two world wars.

This period in the history of American labor was one of the movement finding itself. Unions called attention to the hazards working people faced at the turn of the century, encouraging the American government to establish workplace rules and regulations that most of us take for granted today.

But unions abused their newfound power by calling national strikes that damaged the economy and threatened to shut down entire cities. Lastly, Americans perceived organized labor as endangering the war effort.

By the end of the 1940s, public perception seemed to be that unions were a necessary evil. With a growing membership and increasing power, labor unions were poised to make their move—but whether that move would be good for the working people or labor's advancement remained to be seen....

History of Unions: 1950–Today

As World War II came to a close, unions were riding high, with over 25 percent of American workers carrying union membership cards. The union's wartime promise of refraining from strikes was no longer valid, and strikes became their weapon of choice.

After 1946's Great Strike Wave, something had to give. With over 250 union-related bills pending in both houses of Congress in 1947, the Labor Management Relations Act of 1947 became law. Better known today as the Taft-Hartley Labor Act, President Truman argued that the Act was a "dangerous intrusion on free speech," and Congress enacted it over Truman's veto. History would note that Truman would subsequently use it twelve times during his presidency.

The 1950s brought the Cold War, and communism paranoia was rampant. Labor leaders called Taft-Hartley the "slave-labor bill," while business leaders saw it as a means to curtail the growing power of organized labor.

Unions quickly realized that the long-term ramifications of Taft-Hartley were much larger than they knew. Not only did it amend 1935's National Labor Relations Act, but it also was not going to go away. Labor leader and powerful negotiator Walter Reuther saw the government's growing hostility toward the labor movement.

Reuther saw that politics were going to play a significant role in how unions would operate in the future, and in the face of Taft-Hartley, organized labor would have to work around the rules to control the outcome of legislation with the right candidates in place.

In 1948, as the president of the UAW, Reuther negotiated with General Motors for the first contract ever to include provisions for a "cost of living" wage adjustment. That contract and the one that followed were significant, as they—and Reuther—demonstrated a shift from the unions focusing on working conditions to an emphasis on quality of life for workers and their families.

What's important to understand at this point is that Americans have always had a love-hate relationship with organized labor. Unions themselves had moved to a model that invited corruption and infighting. This new "big business" model, coupled with the abusive power of the strike, heralded a decline in membership during the 1950s, a decline that caused problems for the AFL and the CIO. Not surprisingly, the two organizations began to compete for a declining number of members.

To improve the labor movement's chance of survival in postwar America, new leadership with George Meany, President of the American Federation of Labor, and Reuther, now President of the Congress of Industrial Organizations, made way for an entirely new approach and a true collaboration, creating what we know now as the AFL-CIO. In 1955, union membership was estimated at 35 percent (fifteen million workers), with George Meany as the first president of the combined organization.

Labor leaders saw the government implementing labor laws like the Wagner Act, wage and hour protections, Social Security, and forty-hour workweeks… as well as coercive power directed against labor unions. But politicians suddenly realized that many of the rights that labor unions had been fighting for were politically useful, and politicians began to jump on the bandwagon to champion worker protections.

But it turned out that cooperation wasn't the unions' plan. By the end of the 1950s, a group of union leaders came to the conclusion that the government's involvement wasn't solely for the protection of their members—they began to advance the theory that it was a calculated strategy of corporate management. And the truth was, management was taking a harder line after what had been perceived as "softer" bargaining over the previous decade.

The new corporate bargaining strategy arose with the Eisenhower Recession of 1957–1958. The circumstances of the time allowed management to bargain for more stringent work standards, to discipline workers, and to utilize their workforce in ways they dictated—all of which were seen by unionized workers as possible threats to job security.

The loss of power at the bargaining table translated into losses in private-sector union membership. Despite—or perhaps because of—these membership losses, the 1960s brought a return to trade unionism, as public employee unions rose to power.

In 1962, President Kennedy, by way of an Executive Order, recognized the right of federal workers to bargain collectively. Public sector employees saw the Order as a breakthrough, as 1935's Wagner Act did not protect them. Public sector unions tripled in size—from four million workers in 1950 to twelve million by 1976.

While manufacturing and farming jobs steadily declined in the private sector, a public sector job secured competitive wages, generous benefits, and job security, making possible a stable middle class for nearly everyone. Unions quickly took advantage of public sector bargaining sessions to hold up as an example to gain more members in both public and private sectors. The American Federation of State, County, and Municipal Employees—AFSCME—was just one example of this phenomenal public-sector union growth. From 1964 to 1978, under President Jerome Wurf, AFSCME grew to five times its size, from just 200,000 members to a million.

With a different point of view, Wurf, who aggressively recruited women and African Americans, saw the power of using politics as a vehicle to get what the union wanted. AFSCME created its first political action committee in 1971, supporting George McGovern's 1972 presidential bid. His PAC bolstered Jimmy Carter's successful presidential bid in 1976, and it was an early supporter of Barack Obama's 2008 presidential campaign as well.

The atmosphere of the 1960s saw a rise in activist unionism, and unions sought to grow through efforts to organize groups that were previously thought of as "unable to be organized," including low wage–earning minority workers. That's why the next two decades brought strikes and boycotts led by United Farm Workers labor leader Cesar Chavez.

Chavez made unionization a way of life for migrant farm workers in California, uniting those workers as a movement, an epic struggle for survival. Today, California, Colorado, and Texas celebrate Cesar Chavez Day as a state holiday, but Chavez's movement was truly the exception. Then, as now, unions often served their own interests during negotiations, rather than the greater good of the country and its citizens, a fact that did not escape the government's attention.

The American government began establishing critical public policies regarding a host of worker issues, including full employment or acceptable levels of unemployment. The government created the 1962 Contract Work Hours Standards Act, the Equal Pay Act of 1963, the Civil Rights Act of 1964, worker's compensation laws, and addressed age discrimination in the Employment Act of 1967.

President Nixon's Occupational Safety and Health Act, now commonly referred to as OSHA, was passed during this time as well, with the intent of ensuring that employers would provide employees with an environment free from recognized hazards. Together, these federal policies helped to create a positive atmosphere for all workers.

It became apparent that unions could no longer exclusively focus on collective bargaining, militant action, and strikes, but would have to meet the demands of public interest and policy through politics, as Walter Reuther had foreseen back in the late forties.

The year 1971 brought us the Federal Election Campaign Act, designed to create transparency regarding monetary contributions to federal political campaigns, and to place legal limits on those contributions. But financial restrictions were difficult to enforce because they were easy to circumvent, and labor's involvement in politics only grew and grew.

Multiple political action committees were created to assist in campaign finance reform, tracking any organization that received or spent more than $2,600 for the purpose of influencing a federal election. By 1974, there were 201 union-affiliated PACs, and although PACs can only solicit contributions from their members, ten years later there were over four hundred labor PACs.

In the 1980s, many companies began actively opposing unionization and the constraints and restrictive union contracts unionization could bring. This shift in corporate sentiment was exemplified by the landmark events surrounding 1981's Air Traffic Controllers strike. Nearly thirteen thousand Professional Air Traffic Controllers Organization (PATCO) members went on strike after their union rejected the government's "best and final" offer. In an unprecedented move, President Ronald Reagan threatened the strikers: "Return to work within forty-eight hours, or be fired." The President made good on this threat, not only by firing those who refused to return but by permanently replacing them. The PATCO strike has been called the "strike that busted unions," because Reagan's actions took the bite out of the threat of public-sector union strikes.

A number of other notable strikes in the eighties turned public sentiment against organized labor, including the Major League Baseball strike in 1981. The violent 1983 Phelps-Dodge copper strike and 1985's Hormel Meatpackers' strike led the public to wonder whether strikes were worth their cost. By 1987, the NFL Players' strike and the 1989 Eastern Airlines strike—which resulted in the demise of the airline—confirmed the public's view that strikes were ineffective.

It didn't take long for corporate America to catch on to the new dynamic, and soon private companies saw opportunities to eliminate unions by hiring replacement workers during strikes. Unions called these workers "scabs," and publicly shamed those who crossed the picket lines, which often included their own members.

Throughout the eighties and nineties, organized labor continued to shrink, both in membership and in influence. Jobs were disappearing, and so were unions. Many unions went far outside their core industries to gain new members and survive. Still others chose to merge their way into more dues-paying members.

A good example of these "merge to win" tactics is the Service Employees International Union, under the leadership of John Sweeney. Sweeney became President of the SEIU in 1980 when the union's membership was around 625,000 members. Sweeney pushed for rapid expansion, swallowing up smaller unions and moving into new sectors and industries, including office workers, nursing home workers, and maintenance workers in health-care and business offices.

By 1993, the SEIU was the first AFL-CIO union to reach the million-member mark in more than twenty years. But more than half of the union's growth had come through mergers with smaller unions.

Then, in 1995, riding high on his success with the SEIU, John Sweeney was elected President of the AFL-CIO. And another up-and-coming leader, Andy Stern, took Sweeney's place as the President of the SEIU.

So let's pause to reflect for a moment. At the peak of organized labor, back in 1954, nearly 35 percent of all U.S. workers belonged to a union. But today, that percentage is just less than 7 percent in the private sector.

In the struggle to keep the labor industry afloat, it was perhaps inevitable that, in the late 1990s and the early 2000s, unions would begin turning on each other.

In 2004, still under the leadership of John Sweeney, the AFL-CIO was a federation of fifty-seven unions. While Sweeney had made significant structural changes, he was not able to curtail the rapid decline in union membership. The SEIU, led by Andy Stern, was vocal in expressing that he thought the AFL-CIO should be reformed, or that workers should "build something stronger."

Eventually, this conflict came to a head, and in 2005, Andy Stern led a revolt....

Stern's SEIU left the AFL-CIO to form a new labor federation called Change To Win. This breakaway group of six million members included the Teamsters, the Laborers, the Farm Workers, the Carpenters, the United Food and Commercial Workers, and the newly merged UNITE HERE.

Change to Win hoped to reinvigorate the labor movement, but truthfully the organization's leaders had a hard time just keeping its members happy. Within five years of its inception, the Carpenters had abandoned ship, one-third of UNITE HERE was swallowed up by the SEIU, and the rest of the original Change To Win members went back to the AFL-CIO by 2013.

In their fight for survival during the eighties and nineties, unions openly began operating as big businesses, with member dues as their largest source of income. Using the legacy of unions to gain more dues-paying members is a difficult sell when Gen Y and Millennials know little about unions, as fewer than 8 percent of their Gen X parents were unionized.

New communication tools, like social media and online card signing, are just some of the things that unions are using to try to catch up. Convincing today's workers to join a union continues to challenge organized labor. That's why, in the last decade, unions have returned to Walter Reuther's vision of focusing on legislative efforts to help them survive.

In 2008, community organizer Barack Obama was elected President of the United States. To repay the unions for their strong support in getting him elected, Obama tried to pass the Employee Free Choice Act (or "card check bill") in 2009. The EFCA failed to pass in Congress. History will note that Senator Hillary Clinton (Democrat, New York), the Democratic candidate for President in 2016, cosponsored the legislation.

Still believing in the power of political influence, unions helped to reelect Obama in 2012, and in 2015 the NLRB directly implemented "ambush" election rules and micro-unit campaigns, this time bypassing Congress. These political efforts were designed to boost membership by minimizing the time and money needed for unions to organize new members.

Unions will adapt their strategies to try to prove their relevance in the twenty-first century, creating an even more unstable brand for the big business of organized labor. This instability requires that everyone—unions, workers, and management alike—all be highly informed and ready to respond.

I hope that this in-depth look at the history of organized labor has provided you with new insight into labor unions—insight you'll need to use to prepare your company and educate your workforce.

CHAPTER 2

Why Become Union-Proof?

The Cost of Unionization

Thirty-two percent. That's the estimated average increase in labor costs for a company after unionization. Unionization can affect a business in a variety of ways, including a loss in productivity, lower morale, less innovation, and a lack of focus on the customer.

But even more eye-opening is the financial impact of unionization. Including the costs of bargaining, administration, legal assistance, and even dues coming from the employees themselves, the cost of a unionized operation can become overwhelming.

You may think you understand the added costs of running a business with a unionized workforce, but truth be told, you probably don't know the half of it. You might have a vague understanding that unionizing could lower the company's profit margins, but when it comes to corporate finance today, "guessing" isn't good enough. The real cost of unionization is a subject that must be dealt with in a pragmatic way.

As the world economy continues to remain volatile, union representation may seem more appealing than ever to workers who are concerned about their job security, wages, and benefits—all things related to their company's financial health. Union organizers are smart. If they can't get employees to organize in traditional ways, they'll go after the enterprise's bottom line. So, while your company is working to grow and build up a good reputation in the community and marketplace, unions arrive more than willing to bruise that reputation a bit to successfully gain new dues-paying members. They do this through orchestrated—and potentially expensive—corporate campaigns that are meant to impact the company's reputation.

A corporate campaign is an all-out assault on the company, designed to cost money, lower productivity, and reduce profitability by causing damage to a company's reputation through media, political influence, and a variety of other channels. Corporate campaigns are crafted to call a company's integrity into question in some way.

This fear of upper management seeing profits decline is designed to motivate the company to agree to a union presence—but this is a losing proposition. While a corporate campaign may cost you some customers, a union presence in the company can be far more damaging financially.

However, trying to pin down *exactly how much* unionization can cost a company is often challenging because there are so many variables at play—not the least of which is the fact that the expense of a union doesn't begin when the contract agreement is made, or even when the final vote is tallied. The meter actually starts running the minute a union-organizing drive begins.

Jim Gray, president of Jim Gray Consultants, a firm that specializes in helping business leaders with human resources and business-transitioning issues, found that midsized businesses could expect to spend anywhere from $250,000 to more than $1,250,000 on a single unionization campaign.

These costs include items such as attorneys' fees, travel expenses, meetings with employees, video presentations, lost productivity, and even other intangible elements that are hard to quantify but can add up to thousands—even millions—of dollars lost. This means that the company is experiencing the cost of unionization even before the union is voted in—but once a union is voted in, those costs grow even higher.

How high could they grow? In Dr. Lloyd Field's landmark book, "*Unions Are Not Inevitable,*" he references multiple studies conducted in the five-year period following unionization. The findings, according to Field, demonstrated that a newly organized company's operating costs increased by more than 25 percent of their gross payroll and benefit costs. Field provides an example: The unionization of a company with a gross payroll of $18,000,000 would result in $4,500,000 in *additional* annual operating costs, all thanks to the presence of a union.

And that's just for newly organized companies. In *Union Proof: Creating Your Successful Union-Free Strategy*, author Peter Bergeron, who spent thirty-three years in the field of labor relations and human resources, estimates that the average operating costs of a unionized company could be even higher—25 to 35 percent higher than the cost of running a union-free organization. So, where does that 25 to 35 percent go?

Many people assume that it goes to the employees, to pay for whatever additional wages or benefits the union negotiates on their behalf—and certainly some of that added cost may be the result of these kinds of pay or benefit increases. But about how much money are we *actually* talking?

A study released by the Bureau of Labor Statistics found that union-free employers paid an average of $19.51 per hour in wages and salaries, while union employers, in the same sector, were obligated to pay $23.02 per hour—an added expense of $3.51 per hour. Additionally, union-free employers paid $7.56 per hour in benefits, while the cost for unionized companies' benefits was nearly double—at $14.67.

And these calculations don't even include the cost of unionization for employees, paid in the form of dues, fees, and assessments.

So, while not insignificant, you can see that the outcome of collective bargaining represents just a small percentage of the cost increases involved in running a unionized company.

Another sizeable line item goes toward dealing with the legal and administrative challenges that are presented by integrating the union and its processes into a company's workplace. These might not be the things you immediately think about when considering the costs of a union. The question is "are you ready for this?" The administrative costs of unionization can include:

- More human resources staff
- More employees, due to less flexibility
- More time and money spent discussing overtime policies, grievances, and arbitration
- Increased legal costs
- Time spent dealing with wage and hour laws, OSHA, and the EEOC
- Time spent in collective bargaining and preparing for bargaining
- Time spent in union contract administration training
- Greater seniority administration
- Changes in Company systems and processes in order to better track finances
- Time spent formulating plans for the big "what if?"—including strike contingency planning
- And much, much more...

In addition, many of these costs carry with them an element of unpredictability, which can certainly make any CFO nervous: Contract negotiations, for instance, have no deadline, and they could go on for weeks, months, and even years without ever reaching an agreement. In such a case, when you have your best labor attorneys on the job, the cost to the company can be significant.

Even with all of that, the full impact of the cost of unionization isn't actually realized until you begin factoring in another critical, but often overlooked variable—and that's the effect a union presence can have on a company's market value.

A union presence can make a company less competitive:
- Production may slow due to union rules.
- Contracts can limit a company's flexibility and its ability to meet customer needs.

- There is less opportunity for employees, as union rules can restrict cross-training and personal growth.
- Even the possibility of a union strike can be a turnoff for potential customers and high-performing job candidates.
- Union seniority rules may prevent the best workers from rising to the highest positions, and they may force companies to retain poor performers. This may result in lower quality products, reduced productivity, or both.

In fact, by definition, seniority provisions in union contracts remove most incentives for employees to work harder, or even smarter because there's little reward for above-average performance. This can encourage a mindset of mediocrity in the workplace, which can be very dangerous, especially for companies that operate with razor-thin profit margins, or that work in highly competitive industries.

Such a loss of a company's competitive edge isn't a one-time thing. Extending the research out to ten years' post-unionization, the Employment Policy Foundation concluded that, overall, unless a unionized company was able to sell their products at a higher price, or somehow attain other financial savings, they were likely to see a 14 percent drop in profits as opposed to their non-union competitors.

In a different study, labor researchers David Lee and Alexandre Mas also looked into how unionization affected a company's overall valuation. They found that following a union election victory, companies experienced a decline in market value of about 10 percent. A two-million-dollar company would lose two hundred thousand dollars in value, thus vastly affecting business plans, loans, and credit ratings.

On top of a loss in the company's market value, studies have shown that unionized companies end up investing about 15 percent less in both physical capital and in research and development (R&D) as a direct result of unionization. One study even found that being unionized has the same effect on business investment as a 33 percent increase in corporate income tax!

So, what's the takeaway here? Unionization means higher costs, less flexibility, a less-motivated workforce, less innovation and creativity, lower market value, and less investment back into the business. Taken all together, that makes unionized companies far less competitive than union-free operations in the same industry.

It is important to keep in mind that a loss of flexibility turns into a real cost of unionization when unionized companies need to reduce costs immediately to survive a downturn or bankruptcy.

If you keep an eye on the news, you'll see many stories of companies trying to negotiate with unions to lower their costs and make concessions for the very continuation of the company's existence in the marketplace.

Many times—and legally so—companies can remove a union entirely at this point, just to survive. But on other occasions, the union refuses to cooperate, leading to harder times, or worse, the company actually being forced to shut its doors. As we talk about Job Security, I'll use the story of Hostess and their two unions as an example of this very thing.

Job Security

Today every company, no matter how large or small, operates in a global economy. Businesses are forced to keep prices low—even when their costs are high. Customers expect everything better, cheaper, faster…and if your company can't deliver, there are many other competitors out there who can.

We've come a long way from the customer expectations of the early twentieth century when unions hit their membership peak by making promises of higher wages, better benefits, and job security for all. Despite embracing online communications and a variety of modern organizing tactics, unions are still using this same sales pitch, resting on their accomplishments in the past—but the question we need to ask is: can they actually make good on their promise to protect jobs *today*?

To answer this question, let's start by reviewing some basic economic theory... When the world economy is good, demand for products and services increases and businesses grow by investing in more capital or a larger workforce. Typically, this kind of corporate growth increases job confidence, and with it, job security.

However, when the economy hits a recession, the opposite becomes true. Businesses experience reduced demand, and they must begin looking for ways to cut costs, which can result in downsizing.

The key to fostering job security, then, is to work to keep demand for your product or services high, regardless of the economy, and that's done by remaining competitive. When companies can meet customer demands of better, cheaper, and faster, they're said to be "competitive" in the marketplace—and businesses that are considered "competitive" have a higher rate of job security.

In essence, your company's ability to be competitive is dependent on demonstrating three things of which the entire company needs to be aware: flexibility, added value, and customer focus.

We'll start with *flexibility*. Having flexibility means understanding what your customers need and being able to meet those needs more quickly than your competition. It's about staying nimble, meeting deadlines, going the extra mile, and being the company that can find the right solutions. That kind of flexibility is what gives your company a strong competitive edge.

Unfortunately, unions actually work against that kind of flexibility. Rigid union work rules and red tape could restrict your company's ability to meet customer demands, and they may actually prevent your employees from going the extra mile to help a client, even if they want to. A lack of flexibility can hurt workers, companies, and even whole industries.

In one very visible example, consider a time years ago in this country when almost the entire trucking industry was unionized—but following the Motor Carrier Act of 1980, which deregulated interstate trucking, competition increased and profits decreased, causing nearly two hundred unionized trucking companies to shut their doors.

Unionized trucking companies simply weren't nimble enough. Deregulation of the trucking industry reduced shipping costs—typically passed on to consumers—by anywhere from 8 to 15 percent, and that new competitive landscape meant that the contracts, the corruption, and the disruptions associated with unions all made it hard for unionized trucking companies to stay flexible.

Even more recently, consider the circumstances that led the iconic Hostess Bakery to shut its doors in 2012. While no end of bad business decisions led up to the company's closing, the final nail in Hostess's coffin was undoubtedly the standoff with their two unions.

Already in Chapter 11 bankruptcy, Hostess asked its two biggest unions for new contracts that would allow greater concessions, so that the company would be able to stay afloat. After taking a look at the company's finances, the Teamsters agreed, but the Baker's Union did not. Instead, they chose to strike. While some workers crossed the picket line to try to keep the production line moving, in the end, these efforts weren't enough to save the company.

They couldn't keep up with the customer demand. According to Hostess CEO: "The strike impacted us as far as cash flow. The plants were operating at well below 50 percent capacity, and customers were not getting products." The Hostess name lives on today, thanks to the efforts of its new ownership. Today, it employs 1,800 employees throughout the United States. However, previously its workforce was more than ten times that number, and the reductions were made in both union and non-union bakeries alike.

Had the Baker's Union been more flexible to the needs of the company, Hostess might have ultimately been able to meet the demands of its customers. Without that flexibility and cooperation, the company was sold, and the new owners were forced to lay off 90 percent of Hostess workers—people who probably thought they had some serious job security thanks in part to their union relationship. By their actions, the union not only *didn't* protect the jobs for the unionized workers, but they actually accelerated the company's demise.

Corporate flexibility is clearly crucial in remaining competitive and creating job security for company workers. Now let's talk about the concept of *added value*. "Added value" refers to things that give your brand an advantage over your competitors, and which cause a potential customer to choose to work with your company or purchase your product or service—essentially. Added value is that one thing customers use to differentiate in choosing one company over another.

Think about what gives your company and its products added value in the marketplace. It might be the extras you add in for free or the high quality of your materials, or maybe even your fantastic customer service and the relationships you have established with those people who love your brand. But—and here's where it gets fascinating—it might *also* be the fact that your company is union-free.

Staying union-free can be excellent for your business. We've already seen how union-free companies have more flexibility in meeting customer needs, but union-free companies are often viewed as more responsive and reliable in general. No matter whether you're in a business-to-consumer or a business-to-business environment—your end customer knows that they can count on you. There's no chance of a strike at your union-free facilities; no worries that restrictive union rules will slow down a shipment, and more confidence that the people doing the work are actually the most competent—not just the most senior—members of the team.

Added value in the form of remaining union-free can have a direct effect on customers' decision-making behavior when presented with a competing product or service.

For example, American manufacturing in the United States has been on a decline since the mid-1980s, and manufacturing jobs have declined by a total of 27 percent in that time. But if you isolate *unionized* manufacturing jobs during that period, you'll see that the drop for those companies was a whopping *75 percent*.

Removing unionized companies from our equation presents us with some other great insights into the choices customers make. Clearly, customers will make very specific choices about the kinds of businesses they want to work with or buy from, and the added value a union-free company can provide will affect those decisions.

We've looked at the need for *flexibility*. And we've talked about *adding value* to a company. The third thing your company needs to do to increase job security for its employees is to *focus on the customer*. The company, employees—everyone, really—are in this together. If everyone in the company focuses their energy on taking care of the needs of the customer, then everything else falls into place, including the job security of the company employees.

But what unionized companies often find is that energy that should be spent taking care of the customer is instead devoted to enforcing rules, resolving internal squabbles, and dealing with managers and employees who are many times pitted against one another.

When employees and management cannot work together to maintain a company's profitability, nobody wins—and the customer certainly loses. The American auto industry learned this lesson of *customer focus* the hard way. Over the last several decades, the United Autoworkers Unions and "Big Three" management have been engaged in a bitter and ongoing struggle over contract negotiations—instead of focusing on their customers and at the expense of their product's quality. As they put more and more of their energy into bargaining, they paved the way for foreign automakers to drive right into the American marketplace with competitive products.

When the American economy faced the market crash of 2008, these auto industry giants were forced to accept massive government bailouts just to stay afloat. The car manufacturers and their unions had lost sight of customer focus. Manufacturing and supplier plants were closed, local car dealerships were forced out of business, and thousands upon thousands of American jobs were lost.

Understanding that remaining union-free can be a strong differentiator—especially in times of economic downturn—is vital to the job security of many workers. Customers can and do choose to do business with companies they trust. Because we now operate in a world economy, nothing can actually guarantee job security, but companies that can be flexible, offer their customers added value, and focus their employees' energies on the customer have a better chance at securing long-term viability.

CHAPTER 3

Organized Labor: An Inside Look

The NLRB

To build a union-proof culture, you need to understand the National Labor Relations Board, commonly referred to as the NLRB, including what it is, who it's comprised of, and why even union-free companies need to be aware of the NLRB's reach.

However, it's impossible to discuss the NLRB without considering the law that the Board was established to enforce: The National Labor Relations Act. The National Labor Relations Act (NLRA) was written by Congress back in 1935 to serve as the primary law governing relations between unions and employers in the private sector.

At the time of its writing, it was known as the Wagner Act, after Democrat New York Senator Robert F. Wagner. The NLRA does not cover two main groups of employees: those working for the government and those in the railway or airline industries which are typically covered by the Railway Labor Act. As a foundation for U.S. labor law, the NLRA was enacted to protect the rights of employees and employers. More specifically, the NLRA did the following:
- Legalized the right to strike
- Outlawed the firing of union supporters
- Put management decisions under government scrutiny

- Gave greater freedom to unions
- Placed limits on what an employer could do during a union organizing drive

Not surprisingly, the enactment of the NLRA in 1935 proved to be a boon to union organizing efforts. Within twenty years, 35 percent of the American workforce belonged to a union—but not everyone was happy about it.

Employers felt that the Act was too slanted in favor of unions and union organization, and this sentiment (along with the great wave of disruptive strikes that followed World War II), fueled a movement to amend the NLRA to make it less one-sided.

As I mentioned previously, the Taft-Hartley Act (1947) changed parts of the NLRA, mostly to give more rights to employers, but Taft-Hartley also placed limits on the labor unions' ability to strike.

Then, in the mid-1950s, organized labor came under intense Congressional scrutiny, as many unions had become involved in corruption, racketeering, and other misconduct. Some unions, such as the Teamsters, the International Longshoremen, and the United Mine Workers, became notorious for various illegal activities.

This corruption led Congress to conclude that greater transparency was needed in the unions' activities. The second revision to the NLRA came in 1959, in the form of the Labor-Management Reporting and Disclosure Act—known as the Landrum-Griffin Act.

Landrum-Griffin required unions to:
- Hold secret ballot elections
- Submit annual "LM2" financial reports to the Department of Labor
- Provide certain minimum standards before they could expel or take any other disciplinary action against a member of the union

In the 1960s and '70s, there were a number of failed attempts at further amending the NLRA. In 1978, unions wanted to permit triple back-pay awards to union employees and make union certification based upon signed authorization cards. But since 1959, the NLRA has been left untouched, and it dictates how we govern organized labor today.

Now, you can go online and read the National Labor Relations Act in its entirety if you'd like—but the most relevant section of the Act for you to understand is Section 7, which has been referred to as the "heart" of the NLRA. Section 7 is what you will hear the most about, such as when a "violation of an employee's Section 7 rights" is cited.

Under the Section 7 rule, employees "have the right to self-organization, to form, join, or assist labor organizations to bargain collectively through representatives of their own choosing." They also have the right *not* to join a union, although that right may be affected by an agreement requiring membership in the union as a condition of employment.

Now that you have a basic understanding of the NLRA let's consider the government agency that oversees its enforcement. The National Labor Relations Board was created by Congress in 1935, with the sole purpose to administer and enforce the NLRA.

The NLRB define themselves as an "independent federal agency vested with the power to safeguard employees' rights to organize and to determine whether to have unions as their bargaining representative. The agency also acts to prevent and remedy unfair labor practices committed by private sector employers and unions."

The Board has five primary functions:
- To conduct elections
- To investigate charges
- To facilitate settlements
- To decide cases
- To enforce orders

First, the NRLB oversees and determines, through secret ballot elections, whether private-sector employees wish to organize bargaining units in the workplace or whether they desire to dissolve their labor unions through a decertification election. Second, the Board investigates charges alleging Unfair Labor Practices, or ULPs, filed by employees, union representatives, and employers. Third, when a ULP is determined to have merit, the NLRB encourages the involved parties to resolve cases by settlement rather than litigation whenever possible. Fourth, to assist in deciding cases and passing judgment, the NLRB has approximately forty administrative law judges, known as ALJs, and a board whose five members are appointed by the President and confirmed by the Senate. And finally, the NLRB enforces the orders of decided cases. I should point out that under its statutes, the NLRB cannot assess penalties. However, the agency may seek make-whole remedies, such as reinstatement and back pay for discharged workers, and informational remedies like the posting of a notice by the employer, promising not to violate the law.

With that said, the majority of parties voluntarily comply with the orders of the Board. When they do not, the agency's general counsel must seek enforcement in the U.S. Court of Appeals. Parties with unfavorable decisions may seek review in the circuit or federal courts.

About sixty-five cases a year involving the NLRB are decided in the circuit courts, with nearly 80 percent decided in the Board's favor. Any circuit court decision may be subject to final review by the U.S. Supreme Court if the parties or the Board seek such a review.

Let's take a closer look at the fourth function of the NLRB, and briefly discuss who makes up the actual Board, because its composition is essential for a complete understanding of how the Board does its job.

First, the five Board members function as a quasi-judicial body in deciding cases filed by the parties. The makeup of the Board does sometimes become convoluted, as Board members' terms often overlap and can change at different times. Also, at times appointees are not approved by the Senate quickly—or even at all—meaning there is the possibility that the NLRB must function with fewer than five members. Legally, they must have a minimum of three members to form a quorum to make a decision on a case.

One interesting aspect of the Board is that because members are appointed by the President, politics critically influences each appointment, the same way it affects the makeup of the justices of the Supreme Court. The composition of the five Board members is usually 3–2 in favor of the President's party, with the Chairman of the NLRB typically from that political party. This is important because traditionally, Democratic appointees are more likely to protect labor unions' interests, while Republican members often lean toward the support of the efforts of business and industry. These politics result in a continual swing back and forth by the NLRB, depending on which party is in power when NLRB appointments are made.

The NLRB also has a General Counsel, another appointment made by the president with Senate approval, but only for a four-year term. This position is independent of the Board, and the person is responsible for the investigation and prosecution of any "unfair labor practice" charges, filed by either unions, employees or employers. The General Counsel oversees regional NLRB offices in the processing of these cases.

Remember that the NLRB has no independent power of its own. It can't enforce the orders it gives—any and all enforcement must go through the United States Court of Appeals. What's more, the Board isn't allowed to act on its own—all cases, charges, and election petitions must be initiated by someone else, either an employer, an employee or a union.

That said, the power of the NLRB should never be underestimated. Since its inception in 1935, the decisions made by the NLRB have significantly shaped American labor practices—and when politics swing in favor of organized labor, that can mean tough times for companies like yours that want to stay union-free.

However, of particular interest to you and your company would be what took place in 2009: the introduction of the

Employee Free Choice Act, or the EFCA, to Congress. The EFCA was a legislative bill that was brought before both chambers of Congress on March 10th of that year. The bill's purpose was to amend the NLRA, in order to establish a more efficient system to enable employees to form, join, or assist unions and to provide for mandatory injunctions for ULPs during their organizing efforts.

There are three reasons it's important for you to know about the EFCA:

1. It assumed that after seventy-five years, the NLRA was no longer an efficient system.
2. Instead of promoting free choice, it eliminated the secret ballot election.
3. It tried to limit an employer's ability to communicate and educate employees about unions.

Being a bit too ambitious for its own good, the EFCA failed to pass during the 110th United States Congress. However, the key point to take away from this event is that it was a legislative bill created with union support and the support of political parties, and it was not something brought forth by the NLRB itself; the NRLB can, however, create new rules without going through Congress.

Since the failure of the EFCA in 2009, the NLRB has brought about more changes to unionization than at any time since the NLRA was made into law. The NLRB has flexed its muscles, creating a whole host of new rules and rulings (many still pending) that make it easier for unions to organize workers and harder for employers to stop them from doing so.

Many of these rule changes affect—you guessed it—Section 7 rights.

Because the term *"protected concerted activity"* can be defined in so many different ways, the NLRB has been able to expand its views on what might be considered "concerted activities," and therefore create rules to protect such activities, including those conducted on social media and by e-mail.

The NLRB is now producing rulings that make it easier for unions to organize employees successfully. These new decisions include the advent of "ambush" or "expedited" election schedules, which dramatically reduce the amount of time employees have to learn about unions before they vote on representation. It's now legal for unions to organize an entire company little by little, using "micro-unit elections," in which unions conduct elections with just a few employees at a time.

As bad as these new rules are, they are not the only danger to companies like yours. Handbook policies of union-free employers have come under increased scrutiny, based on the NLRB's reinterpretation of "protected concerted activity," for any policies that could include potential violations of Section 7 rights.

Recently, the NLRB's Office of the General Counsel discussed a case regarding employee handbook policies in which "under the Board's decision… the mere maintenance of a work rule may violate Section 8(a)(1) of the Act if the rule has a chilling effect on employees' Section 7 activity"…is unlawful. As a result of this potential "chilling effect," union-free employers are now facing charges of unfair labor practices. Policies that were previously deemed acceptable are now being considered illegal under this new lens of scrutiny.

Clearly, you've got to be on your toes, as the NLRB's newer interpretations of the NLRA can cause headaches for union-free employers. Understanding these new rules and then combating the threat of the new election rules means that you've got to be proactive. Make sure that your company is educating your employees about unions before they become a target—because, by design, there simply won't be time for education once a unionization campaign begins.

Corruption

"To research the issue of corruption in America's labor unions is both exhilarating and exasperating. Few experiences are more satisfying than

reading and then writing about organized labor's embezzlers and extortionists getting their just deserts. Yet despite all of the expulsions, arrests, indictments, and convictions, there is also despair. For the story too often stays the same even if the cast of characters changes. Corruption remains deeply embedded in the ways unions supposedly represent dues-paying workers."
—From *Union Corruption in America: Still a Growth Industry* by Carl F. Horowitz

Most of the time, when you talk about the labor movement, the words *"corruption,"* and *"union"* go hand in hand. People think of organized crime, of pension plans going broke overnight, even of the disappearance of Jimmy Hoffa—and for good reason. After all, the term *racketeering* isn't meant to describe crimes committed solely by organized labor, and yet it's almost exclusively used to describe just that. It's important for you, as part of your company's union-proofing team, to understand of what, exactly unions have been—and are still—capable.

While there's no globally accepted definition of the word, in most discussions, *corruption* is defined as "the abuse of power or position in order to acquire personal benefit." When it comes to systemic corruption within labor unions, it can include bribery, embezzlement, theft, fraud, extortion, and even blackmail. It also may include corrupt gains, such as abuse of discretion—that is, when someone misuses their powers and decision-making abilities for their personal gain. Favoritism and nepotism are a prime example, for they don't benefit the perpetrator but instead benefit someone related to them, like a friend, family member, or associate.

Now, of course, we all understand that union corruption and union violence are not the same things, but they are mutually reinforcing, and they have been a part of organized labor since its inception. And so, for the better part of the last century, our legal system has attempted to combat both of these practices through legislation, followed by investigation and prosecution.

Criminals began to infiltrate some labor unions in the 1930s when the end of Prohibition cut mob revenues. Mobsters utilized unions to extort money from employers and to help themselves to workers' pension funds. To counter this corruption, legislative efforts began with the Copeland Anti-Kickback Act of 1934. Senator Royal S. Copeland headed up a Senate subcommittee on crime, which found that that up to 25 percent of federal money paid for labor, typically union labor, was actually returned by the employees as a kickback to their employing contractors. In response, the Copeland Act made it unlawful to cause someone to give up their compensation —by force, intimidation, threat of dismissal, or any other coercive method. The 1946 Hobbs Act followed, involving legislation aimed directly at those who committed acts of union corruption and racketeering. It threatened fines and incarceration for:

- Obstructing, delaying, or affecting commerce,
- By robbery or extortion, or by
- Committing or threatening to commit physical violence against people or property.

One year later, the Taft-Hartley Act came into being, amending the NLRA "…to eliminate practices that have the potential for corrupting the labor movement." The Act was significant because it made it a federal crime for employers to give or lend anything of value to unions or their officials, or for a labor official to demand or accept anything of value from an employer. It also prohibited "featherbedding," which is just a nice way of describing the "payment of someone for services not performed or the hiring of more workers than is required."

The Copeland Act, the Hobbs Act, and the Taft-Hartley Act all made great strides for the country in limiting the impact of union corruption, but they certainly didn't put an end to it.

The 1950s brought a great example of corruption with John Dioguardi, or Johnny Dio, an Italian-American known as a racketeer and infamous figure in organized crime. He was appointed the regional director of the UAW along with twelve charters of paper locals in the New York garment industry.

What's a "paper local"? It's a local union with no or few members, chartered by an existing union and formed for the purpose of criminal activity. Johnny's criminal friends, as the members of these paper locals, went around and demanded money from any employers who wished to remain union-free, as well as extorting cash from unionized companies who wanted to avoid strikes and other labor issues.

In 1955, Johnny ran the same scheme with seven more paper locals for the Teamsters, a reward for helping Jimmy Hoffa oust then–Teamsters President Dave Beck. His reign of corruption carried into the 1960s.

In that same year, 1955, the AFL and the CIO merged to form the fifteen-million-member powerhouse union known today as the AFL-CIO. Not long after this merger took place, they pushed out Jimmy Hoffa and the Teamsters, the Bakery Workers, and the Laundry Workers, due to corruption. All of this labor racketeering gave the Republicans a chance to steal the working-class vote away from the Democrats. In 1957, appointed by President Dwight Eisenhower, Senator John L. McClellan and Chief Counsel Robert F. Kennedy ran the largest congressional investigation of its time, making Jimmy Hoffa its target and the poster boy for labor racketeering.

The Committee on Improper Activities in Labor- Management Affairs brought about such publicity and revelations that they ultimately undercut the entire labor movement. Polls showed increasing disdain for unions, and their leaders in particular. Hoffa was eventually forced out by his own union; he went to prison for fraud and jury tampering, was pardoned by Nixon five years later...and then famously disappeared in 1975.

The growing resentment inspired by the Committee hearings helped conservatives win a new round of legislative restrictions on organized labor starting in 1959 with the

Labor-Management Reporting and Disclosure Act, referred to as the Landrum-Griffin Act. The Labor-Management Reporting and Disclosure Act prohibited:

- Anyone from using force, violence, or threats to intimidate a union member from exercising their rights
- Union officers or union employees from embezzling or stealing union monies
- Union officers or union members from engaging in picketing for the purpose of personal profit or gain

A little over ten years later, the Organized Crime Control Act of 1970 brought about RICO, the Racketeer Influenced and Corrupt Organizations Act. RICO was drafted to combat organized crime's infiltration into legitimate economic enterprises.

The RICO ACT aided the FBI in making labor racketeering a priority, because, as they would later report: "Labor racketeering has become one of the fundamental sources of profit, national power, and influence for the Italian-American Organized Mafia, known as the Cosa Nostra."

Finally, the Employment Retirement Income Security Act was enacted in 1974, making bribery and embezzlement of union pensions and welfare funds a federal crime. In the years since, some individual state laws have also been enacted, to protect against racketeering, organized crime, and union corruption.

Racketeering continues to be romanticized in the media, in movies, and in television shows like *The Sopranos*, in which organized crime's connection to unions required no explanation by the show's writers. But the reality of this regard, and of union corruption in general, is anything but romantic. Today it would be hard to find a union that hasn't experienced some form of corruption within its ranks—but a handful of unions seem to have perfected it into an art form.

In fact, four unions were identified in 1986 by Ronald Regan's executive order—the President's Commission on Organized Crime—as being, above all others, "...substantially influenced and/or controlled by organized crime...." Those four unions were the Teamsters, the Laborers, H.E.R.E., and the Longshoremen's Association.

In the wake of the Commission's report, all four of these unions faced some level of additional oversight:

- The Justice Department filed a massive RICO suit against the Teamsters in 1989, citing decades of "pervasive" control of the union by organized crime. Facing multiple racketeering convictions, Teamster officials agreed to place their union under government supervision by an independent review board.
- The Hotel Employee and Restaurant Employees Union found themselves in a similar situation, with the federal government supervising their operations for the next five years.
- The Laborers escaped a civil RICO suit by agreeing instead to an eleven-year self-policing arrangement;
- The Longshoremen managed to avoid federal oversight by being proactive and hiring an "independent ethical practices counsel" to root out corruption in its own union.

It's important to note that organized crime is not behind every corrupt act that union officials and members commit. In fact, most instances of union corruption—for all unions, not just these four—do not typically involve organized crime. But corruption continues nonetheless. According to the Center for Union Facts, in just the last five years, hundreds, and maybe even thousands, of labor leaders—at all levels of the movement—have been convicted of embezzlement, corruption, racketeering, or engaging in organized crime. Many officials feel that corruption is still rampant—and even getting worse—and that union leaders are refusing to address it, except for Jimmy Hoffa Jr....

In early 2015, after twenty-five years of U.S. government oversight, Jimmy Hoffa Jr. said: "As a result of the dedication and strength of our members, I can finally say without hesitation that corrupt elements have been driven from our union and that government oversight can come to an end." After *twenty-five years...*

On NPR, Robert Fitch, the author of a book entitled *Solidarity for Sale*, described today's unions as "classically corrupt." And the use of the word "classically" here is crucial to your understanding of why corruption is still prevalent today. Fitch, who was once a labor union organizer, explains what he calls the "Fiefdom Model of Unions," which works like this: In any union organization, you have a union boss who controls the union staff jobs and sometimes the direct hiring in the industry. If you're a union staffer, you depend on that boss for your livelihood. If you're a union member, he may also be responsible for your livelihood, by getting you industry jobs. So… if that union boss begins dipping into the health-care fund, starts getting kickbacks from the pension fund, or involves himself in some kind of shady racket, as a union staffer or a union member, you may feel compelled to turn a blind eye to his activities, because you have to have a way to provide for your family.

Fitch summed it up this way: "It's a union model that represents the Middle Ages much more than modern capitalism."

Let's now take a quick look at the "politicization of union corruption," to quote NYU School of Law professor James Jacobs. In a recent research study of union corruption, which Jacobs titled, "Is Labor Union Corruption Special?" he goes all the way back to 1988 and mentions "…the firestorm of high-profile opposition from politicians and labor leaders regarding the filing of the blockbuster civil RICO lawsuit against the Teamsters Union.…" The study details the lawsuit's denouncements by people as politically varied as Detroit Mayor Coleman Young, who denounced the lawsuit as a "danger to the freedom of the American people," and AFL-CIO President Lane Kirkland, who said that the RICO lawsuit didn't "sound to me like the proper relationship between government and a private institution in a free society." Senator Orrin Hatch said that the RICO lawsuit flew "in the face of democratic principles" and smacked "of totalitarianism." Congressman Jack Kemp observed that "the United States government is not meant to be in the business of taking things over.… It shouldn't take over your union."

Senator Paul Simon said that the RICO lawsuit against the Teamsters "ought to frighten every American," and Ohio Governor Richard Celeste called the lawsuit "just plain wrong."

What's most fascinating, though, is the fact that in spite of the Teamsters' notorious connection to organized crime, and despite the fact that the politicians had not yet seen the Department of Justice's complaint, 264 members of Congress delivered a petition to the U.S. Attorney General, urging that the Department of Justice *not* file the RICO lawsuit.

The bottom line is that corruption has plagued the labor movement since it began. Efforts to stop corruption have done little to contain it, in some cases actually driving it deeper underground. What's important to understand today is that corruption happens. Not everywhere and not all the time...but we must understand that the culture of unions is a culture that encourages stretching the truth or bending the rules to win at any cost—and this is a very real risk when it comes to organizing union drives.

"Graft and corruption are symptoms of the illness that besets the labor movement, not the cause of it. The cause is the enormous economic and political power now concentrated in the hands of union leaders."
—Barry Goldwater

Union Finances

Forget "grassroots campaigns"—today's unions make a huge amount of money from their members. If you've spent any amount of time studying unions, you know you've got to forget what you've seen in movies or on TV. Unions are not charities, and they're not in it just to make the world a better place. If that were the case, they wouldn't charge workers for their services.

The truth is, unions are multimillion- and sometimes even multibillion-dollar businesses, and they make their money from the monthly dues, initiation fees, and assessments they charge their members. A study by the National Bureau of Economic

Research along with Rutgers University showed that the American union movement was the richest in the world, with assets of $2.6 billion in 1969. To understand the significance of that number, one only had to compare it to the assets of the British union movement (the oldest in the world) which had only $300 million, or the Canadian unions, at $220 million for the same period.

Another interesting analogy in the study presented unions as a "big business." If we were to have merged all U.S. unions into a "conglomerate enterprise," fictitiously called Labor Incorporated, it would have ranked a very real #27 on the Fortune 500.

Ninety percent or more of union revenue is dependent on recurring income—dues. So the only way for unions to increase revenue is by organizing more members, and, of course, it's in a union's best interest to keep their membership numbers growing. Over the last several decades, however, that additional revenue hasn't been so easy to generate. Just fifty years ago, about one-third of U.S. workers belonged to a union. Today, just a little over one in ten workers belongs to a union. And if you look at just the private sector, the decline becomes even more dramatic—less than 7 percent of private-sector workers belong to a union. Because member dues are the prime source of revenue for unions, this drop in membership has had a dramatic impact on unions and their ability to operate the way they always have, to support themselves, if you will, in the way to which they've become accustomed. You would think that if there were ever a time for belt-tightening in unions, it would be now and yet, on the whole, union spending remains high.

On what sorts of things do unions spend their money? Let's find out, based on an LM-2, an annual financial report the government requires all unions to file with the U.S. Department of Labor. LM-2s are public documents, and each year, because of the Freedom of Information Act, the Department of Labor posts them online for anyone who wishes to review them.

Let's break down an LM-2. What you'll find there is a wealth of information about a union's fiscal stability—the money they made that year, and the money they spent, sometimes revealed over hundreds of pages. These expenses are summarized on the right-hand side of Statement B, under the header "Cash Disbursements." Within the categories listed, you'll find the kind of expenses you'd expect—organizing costs, office rental costs, postage, and the like. But, if you look through the whole document, you might find things that surprise you, like multimillion-dollar real estate investments, excessive convention costs, and exorbitant political contributions to various candidates.

The stereotype of union "fat cats" living large on their union members' dime is nothing new—but to see it actually filed in official paperwork can be unsettling. Just how "fat" are these "cats"? Well, let's take a look at some notable purchases disclosed in various LM-2s.

First, there's Linden Hall, a 785-acre estate nestled in the scenic Laurel Highlands of Pennsylvania. This resort includes the mansion itself, a golf course, a swimming pool, and a conference center. Linden Hall was built in 1913, and it features elaborate Victorian furnishings, Oriental carpeting, signed Tiffany windowpanes, and even an Aeolian pipe organ, one of only three that exist in the world today. In 1976, Linden Hall was purchased and restored to its original grandeur by none other than the United Steelworkers of America.

Next, there's the Black Lake Conference Center, a retreat located in Onaway, Michigan. Sitting on a thousand heavily wooded acres on the shore of Black Lake, the resort comes complete with a swimming pool and an 18-hole golf course designed by one of golf's most acclaimed architects, Rees Jones. Reportedly valued at $33,000,000, this peaceful and pricey retreat is owned by the United Auto Workers Union. In fact, in 2015, after the UAW convinced its members to ratify their new contract at the Ford Motor Company, the UAW sent its bargaining team and their families to "staff training" at the four-star Eden Roc Resort in Miami Beach, Florida, rather than using their own multimillion-dollar conference center in Michigan.

And one more: the exclusive Westin Diplomat Resort and Spa, located in Hollywood, Florida, with Art Deco features and hotel suites overlooking the ocean, a golf course, and an infinity pool. It is the peak of Florida luxury. The hotel was purchased in 1997 by the Plumbers and Pipefitters Union for $44,000,000, and they proceeded to spend $800,000,000 of union member pension funds to tear down this beautiful piece of architecture and rebuild it as a thirty-nine-story resort. Mismanagement of its construction led to the United States Labor Department suing the pension fund trustees for failing to manage their members' money properly. In 2014, the union sold the property at a loss of more than $300,000,000.

These property purchases may seem excessive, but they're not the only outrageous purchases you'll uncover in a union's LM-2. From extravagant resorts to private jets, union officials typically enjoy the kind of lifestyles that few of their members could ever hope to afford.

Like even buying Learjets. LM-2s show that the Machinists Union have paid more than $1,500,000 for Learjets, including pilots and maintenance—and they weren't the only ones. The Boilermakers Union partially own two jets, and the International Union of Bricklayers has owned a jet, as well.

Conventions and meetings are opportunities for union officials to enjoy the high life, with planned affairs held at countless golf resorts and high-profile vacation spots like Las Vegas, Puerto Rico, and Hawaii. In 2007, the Teamsters spent $55,000 on gourmet steaks. In 2011, the UAW spent nearly $10,000 on an outing to Six Flags. And the Boilermakers have enjoyed perks like "pheasant hunting expeditions and fly-fishing adventures in Alaska." Most of these events were exclusive—for union executives only—and all of these events were paid for, at least in part, by union members' dues.

Sometimes the outrageous part of union spending is not what they spend their money on, but how much they actually spend. For example, consider the wages that unions pay their executives.

No one has a problem with the fact that they pay their management well for the work they do—the problem comes with just how well unions pay, in the amount that they choose to pay them. Remember, a frequent union tactic is pointing out how much corporate CEO salaries are compared to the workers of a company, as published on the AFL-CIO "Paywatch" website.

But let's see how these union executive salaries compare to the wages of the average dues-paying member:

- The head of the National Production Workers Union was paid a salary of over $591,000 a year.
- The Boilermakers president earned $506,000 a year.
- The Laborers president made $441,000 a year.
- The treasurer of the Teamsters took home $435,000 a year.
- It appears that the leader of the Transportation Communications Union made only $300,000—but upon further review of their LM-2, with business expenses, that figure bumped up to a whopping $750,000.

Executives are not the only ones highly paid in the unions. When combined with the salaries of other union employees, along with office and administrative personnel, their salaries represent 50 percent to 60 percent of recurring disbursements in a typical union's LM-2. One thing you should know is that many unions regularly outspend their income. It's disturbing how common it is for unions to spend all or even more than what they take in, year after year, with seemingly no effort taken to reduce their expenses. With such inflated spending habits as these, it's enough to make you wonder how exactly they manage to stay in business.

Is this "fiscal responsibility"? That's precisely the question that the Mackinac Center for Public Policy asked during a recent study. The Mackinac Study was a systematic review of union spending based on LM-2 reports. It examined six unions—with both public and private sector unions included. Their goal was to determine whether or not unions were acting as responsible stewards of the mandatory dues they collected from their members.

According to the Mackinac researchers: "Our examination indicates that a relatively small amount of union dues money is actually used to represent workers. At best, the picture that emerges from many LM- 2 forms is one of bloated, directionless union organizations with excessive overhead and administrative costs." That's quite a statement!

The study went on to evaluate the effectiveness of the forms, actually finding them barely adequate in overseeing union spending, stating that, "loose definitions and the absence of independent verification, combined with a strong motivation for union officials to obscure political activity and inflate representation, have led to a number of irregularities." Even with LM-2 forms, no one is really getting a complete picture of what unions are spending.

Let's go back to the study by the National Bureau of Economic Research and consider the expenditure line called "on behalf of individual members." In 1962, collectively the LM-2 totals showed that unions spent $18,000,000 "on behalf of individual members"; by 1969 it was $2,100,000, and today it typically shows either nothing at all or mere pennies spent per member.

What spending do the Mackinac researchers believe unions were trying to hide the most? The answer is *political spending*. Unions and politics have always influenced one another—but in recent years, as the decline in union membership continues, political power has become even more essential to the survival of the labor movement.

When union-friendly politicians are in power, legislative bodies like the NLRB are more likely to be populated by union-friendly board members who are more liable to make judgments or laws that make it easier for unions to succeed. That's why labor unions lend their support to handpicked political candidates, those whom they think will repay them by supporting their efforts to make the organization of new members faster and less costly. In 1996, Leo Troy, a profession of economics at Rutgers, estimated that union political spending, across all unions, totaled about

$500,000,000 per political cycle. Just eight years later, an analysis by the National Institute for Labor Relations Research (NILRR) showed that that figure had jumped to $924,000,000.

Continuing forward to the 2011–2012 cycle, the figure balloons to $1,700,000,000, that's 1.7 billion dollars. To put that in perspective, if unions collectively were running for president, they would have outspent the Obama campaign by more than two-to-one. But what's most important for you to understand here is who supplied a hefty portion of that 1.7 billion dollars—union members: union members who are given no say in how their dues money is spent and who are certainly given no say in which candidates their dollars will go to support.

These realizations have left a significant number of people unhappy with the unions. According to a benchmark study of the election-year attitudes of union employees by the Word Doctors, 66 percent of government and private union members said that it was unreasonable for union leaders to spend their dues on political activities without first gaining their approval. Another poll by Zogby showed that 61 percent of unionized employees agreed that union members shouldn't be forced to subsidize political contributions. While union members do, currently, have the right to abstain from paying dues for political activism, another poll demonstrated that 67 percent of workers had no idea that they had the right to withhold mandatory dues for political contributions, a component of what's commonly known as Beck Rights.

(McLaughlin & Associates poll)

On an LM-2, there is a line specifically for a union's annual political contributions, but as the Mackinac Center discovered, the unions have found ways to cleverly—or not-so-cleverly—hide some of those contributions in other places within the form, and so the dollar figures may not necessarily tell the whole story. To be honest, we can't expect them to because a significant amount of union financial activity is not covered by the LM-2 reports. The LM-2 doesn't include contributions to political action committees, or to union benefit or health-care benefit funds, or to any number of other causes about which unions would rather not be asked.

In the end, it's the union members who are losing out, who are paying for those jets and junkets, for the big salaries and the conventions and political campaign contributions—without having any say in how their money is being spent.

Union Constitutions

A *constitution* is a statement of the basic principles and laws of a nation, a state, or an organization, such as a union. The very act of writing a constitution is supposed to clarify an organization's purpose and define the basic structure of the group. The idea is that with a constitution in place, everyone will have a reference point for what the organization is all about and how it operates.

Theoretically, that's the function union constitutions are supposed to serve as well—but how successful are they, as a whole, in reaching those goals?

The union constitution has its roots in the National Labor Relations Act, which recognizes the right of unions to establish and enforce its rules of membership. These rules are outlined in each union's constitution—usually comprised of several hundred pages.

Local unions often have supplemental rules, called "bylaws." These bylaws are the constitution of the local union. Together, the constitution and bylaws outline the different roles of the union officials, with the constitution defining the considerable powers of the international union president and its officers, and the bylaws doing the same on the local level. The constitution usually details how member dues are to be paid, along with assessments and fees and the requirements to remain a member "in good standing." Both the constitution and the bylaws are legally binding documents for union members, so understanding what's in them—and how that content can impact members—is vital. There's just one small problem. It's nearly impossible for potential union members to understand what's in these documents if they don't have easy access to them. Sometimes it's just as difficult to obtain a copy of a union constitutions even if you are already a union member!

Take the case of Glenn Sand, a rank-and-file member of the International Brotherhood of Electrical Workers.... Glenn was a retired IBEW member, and in 2005 he launched a "free speech" website for rank-and-file members about the union. It was called "MyIBEW.net." The site included a discussion forum, information on legal rights, a calendar of IBEW events, and contact information for union officials. It included an online version of the IBEW constitution, one that he'd converted, proofread, and posted online. He'd even added an index that didn't exist in the original document, as well as a search function so that his readers could easily access the information they needed. But when IBEW leadership found out what he was doing, they told him in no uncertain terms that he was "neither authorized nor permitted to publish the IBEW Constitution."

They went on to say that "the International Brotherhood of Electrical Workers is, and must remain, the only official source for the IBEW Constitution." And yet, to this day, if you go on to the IBEW's International website and search for the constitution, you'll find this statement instead: "No Results Found."

This whole situation was well-documented in the Association for Union Democracy's article, entitled "Whose 'IBEW' Is It? An Electrician on the Internet." The article reports that the IBEW isn't alone in these issues. Both in the United States and in Canada, unions have become particularly aggressive in trying to claim the union constitution as their exclusive property.

The IBEW later explained that they "would be happy to send a copy of the constitution to anyone who requests one," but if anything, that offer makes it seem all the more ominous, prompting questions such as: Why do they need to know who is accessing this document? And what's in the constitution that they don't want members to see?

This is a simple issue of union democracy. Union members should have access to information about their union. Union representatives should provide members with current and complete copies of the labor contract, the constitution, and its bylaws—and they should be made readily available on union websites.

But not all unions choose to follow these democratic procedures. So what's really in a union constitution? The website www.1-888-no-union.com performed a rather in-depth analysis of the IBEW constitution to see what exactly the union might have been trying to hide from its membership by keeping their access to the document on a request-only basis. What they found was unsettling. Throughout the document, the union reinforces its control over its members by:

- Claiming jurisdiction over all electrical workers
- Stating and restating that the constitution is "absolutely binding" on all local unions and their memberships
- Referring to the constitution as a "contract" between the union and its members
- Requiring members to take an oath, agreeing to obey the constitution
- Forbidding members from doing any work coming under the IBEW's jurisdiction, be it for pay or for free
- Forbidding members from working for any employer considered to be "in difficulty" with the IBEW. (The phrase "*in difficulty*" is not defined by the IBEW.)

How is a union constitution able to forbid its members from working specific jobs? Well, along with explaining union officials' roles and outlining dues structures, union constitutions describe the rules and regulations that union members are expected to abide by, frequently both on and off the job.

Additionally, some constitutions make a point of mentioning that dues collection from members is enforceable by law, and most contain sections detailing the consequences that can occur when union members break union rules. Let's take a look at some "union member–friendly" headers from the UAW's constitution:

- Trials of Members
- Discipline of Local Members
- Offenses, Penalties, Trials, and Appeals
- Discipline and Expulsion

The offenses outlined in these sections may be described in detail, including specific acts of criminality or corruption, or they may be as vaguely referenced as "engaging in conduct unbecoming a member of the union"—which could include anything disliked by the union.

The IBEW constitution includes a section entitled "Misconduct, Offenses, and Penalties," which outlines what it deems to be punishable offenses, including:

- Violating any of the union rules
- Failing to press charges against a member who violates the rules
- Attempting to kick the union out, or trying to switch unions
- Engaging in acts contrary to a member's "responsibility to the IBEW."
- Working for a company whose "position is adverse or detrimental to the IBEW."
- "Wronging" a fellow union member

The traditional forms of union discipline include suspension, expulsion, and imposing monetary fines or assessments against the individuals who are found guilty. Wondering how much these fines and assessments could cost union members? In the 2014 LM2 for the Teamsters, the "Receipts" line for "Fees, Fines, Assessments, and Work Permits" shows that figure at $4,021,630!

Can unions actually collect on their disciplinary fines? Ask the 143 Boeing employees who crossed picket lines in an eighteen-day strike with 1,900 production and maintenance workers at a New Orleans plant. The International Association of Machinists found all of the strikebreakers guilty, fined them $450 each, and barred them from holding any union office for five years. The charges? Violating the IAM constitution through "improper conduct of a member" and—to paraphrase—"by accepting employment in an establishment where a strike exists."

The Boeing case went all the way to the U.S. Supreme Court...which, eight years later, ruled in favor of the union. Based on the assumption that a union contract is enforceable in state court under the principles of state contract law the court determined that a lawsuit to collect a strike fine, is, at its core, a simple breach-of-contract action.

No one is more familiar with any of this than Stephen Beard, a striking UPS worker and Teamsters member who spoke out against the strike during a media interview. He was found guilty and hit with a $10,000 fine from his union. Teamsters officials said that Beard violated a part of his union membership agreement (constitution) that kept him from impeding negotiations or harming his fellow Teamsters.

Unions like to talk about the power that they can bring to a workplace—but the truth is, the only power a union has is power over its members, and that power is spelled out in each union's constitution and its local bylaws. You can see that when a workplace experiences a union-organizing drive, it's important to educate employees about unions, then empower them to get all the facts—include gaining access to the union's constitution.

If you can, access any union's constitution and read it from cover to cover. You will immediately find that it is one of the most complicated documents you may ever encounter. This is by design. The entire document is written in legalese, with little regard for clarity or ease of reading for the average worker. Think about any lease or mortgage contract you've ever signed, and remember how little language was considerate of you, the buyer. Rather, it was so much more about protecting the seller. It is the same with union constitutions. Employees and potential union workers may be surprised to learn how the majority of the document contains language about what the unions *"will do to them"* as opposed to what the unions *"will do for them."*

CHAPTER 4

Union Organizing

The Four Ways Unions Can Get into a Company

Being union-proof doesn't mean that your business will never be challenged by a union. Odds are, it will happen, sooner or later. What being union-proof does mean is that when the challenges do come, you are prepared. Your employees are already well-informed. You and your team are ready, willing, and able to withstand an organizing drive—confident that you will remain union-free.

There has never been a more critical time for unions to organize than right now. As membership numbers continue to decline, each organizing campaign becomes more and more vital to the survival of the labor movement as a whole. Let's break down the paths that unions can follow to secure the right to represent your workers. It's a little like taking a sneak peek into the other team's playbook. Let's start by identifying some things that three out of the four paths have in common.

Union organizing campaigns begin with the physical arrival of union organizers in your community, or their virtual arrival via the internet. Regardless of how they initiate their first contact, these organizers are hoping for the same thing: to connect with your employees. They may talk with them in the parking lot at work, chat with them online, invite them to a union meeting, or even approach them at their homes.

The goal of these connections is to get workers to sign simple-looking union authorization cards or petitions—but these documents, both the paper versions and the ones found online, are far more complex than they might seem at first glance. Three of the four paths to unionization begin with the collection of signed union authorization cards. Now, unions may tell workers that the card is "harmless"—just a simple piece of paperwork that allows them to share information about unions, or to get the employees an election ballot—but you to need to make sure your employees know that that's not the entire truth.

An authorization card or petition is actually a legally binding document, and a worker's signature or e-signature on one signifies their desire to actually be represented by the union—not their wish to get more information, not their willingness to hold an election—but their desire for union representation, period. And that's why it's so important for your employees to understand the value of their signature. Nowhere on the card does it say that by signing, the employee agrees to give up their right to speak for themselves, directly to management, about their job.

By obtaining your employees' home addresses and telephone numbers, the union can contact your employees at home. It might be with literature or flyers or even bothersome phone calls. Or it might be annoying union organizers coming to their door in person, trying to get more information on the company as well as names and contact information of other employees who might sign cards. The union may ask for the employee's job classification and current wage so the organizer can get a picture of how much the company pays its workers. And, no matter how much the company pays employees, the organizer will likely promise more. Here's a campaign tip: Have your team members ask the organizer to guarantee their pledges in writing and see what happens.

The employee's signature on this legal and binding document is final. If the employee changes his or her mind, the union is under no obligation to return the card. And a signed authorization card is valid for an entire year from the date the employee signs it.

Paper authorization cards have long been labor's standard method for collecting signatures. But with the rise of digital and social media, unions are now embracing the internet as a convenient means of getting the signatures they need. Unions can now legally get employee signatures via the Internet through their union, campaign, or corporate campaign websites.

Some unions have begun using online authorization cards, or "A-Cards," with the employer section often already filled out. Employees are then prompted to enter the following information:
- Name and home address
- E-mail address
- Phone numbers
- Work location or base
- Shift
- Employee ID number

Now that you understand what an authorization card is, both online and off, let's look at how unions use them to organize your employees. The path toward union representation with which you may be the most familiar is the secret ballot election.

Regulated by the National Labor Relations Board, the secret ballot election was designed to give every worker the right to vote on whether or not they wish to be represented by a union.

In the simplest overview, here's how it works: Union organizers arrive, start handing out cards, and begin recruiting your employees to help. If union organizers can get more than 30 percent of the workers to sign an authorization card, petition, or online "A-Card"—even if the workers aren't really interested in joining a union—that union then has the right to request a secret ballot election. The NLRB sets a date for the election, and the vote is held.

Today's election rules require that the company hand over to the union a list of every employee's personal contact information, including e-mail addresses and all relevant phone numbers.

"Expedited" elections also mean that the time frame from petition to unionization can take as few as three weeks and if the union can get enough votes—just 50 percent plus 1 of those who vote—then the union becomes the workers' representative to management.

One key campaign tip is to note the wording I have just shared with you: "50 percent plus 1 of <u>those who vote</u>." It's critical for every eligible employee in the voting unit to vote. Many times, some employees do not want to get involved, and thus they don't bother voting; at that point, just a few (*those who vote*) can determine the outcome for everyone.

Here's another campaign tip: Unions cannot win with 30 percent of the vote, so they typically do not ask or petition for an election if only 30 percent of the cards are signed. They will want to have 50 to 60, or even 75 percent or more of the cards signed before trying to force an election.

Secret ballot elections are a relatively straightforward process, allowing every employee to have a say in the outcome regardless of whether or not they signed an authorization card. But this process troubles unions for a number of reasons, not the least of which is the fact that it actually requires the union to convince workers to vote for them.

Secret ballot elections can also be troubling to unions merely because they're secret—workers are free to vote in private without coercion from either side. Even if an employee signed an authorization card, their vote is still private and employees are then free to vote either way.

Even with unions winning secret ballot elections nearly 70 percent of the time, they will never be satisfied with their success rate. Joe Crump, an official with a United Food and Commercial Workers local union, once wrote: "Employees are complex and unpredictable. Employers are simple and predictable." That's why many unions today are looking to organize employers, not employees. Look at the "Fight for $15" campaign today, and you see an entire industry being organized, not the employees.

This is why increasing numbers of unions are opting for the second path to unionization, one that can sometimes catch companies by surprise because it conveniently sidesteps the secret ballot election process altogether. This method is called Card Check.

For the Card Check process, the path is similar to the secret ballot election process with one exception. Organizers show up, physically, virtually, or both, and start looking for employee support and signatures. But in this case, they don't stop at 30 percent of the workers. This time, they will recruit your employees to get each other to sign up, and they don't stop collecting cards until they get 50 percent or more of your employees to sign a card. If union organizers can get a majority of your workers to sign an authorization card, the union is then allowed to demand "automatic recognition" of the union by the employer. This is called Card Check, and this is how a union can become the workers' representative *without* there ever being an election. In some states, that could mean that employees are forced to join the union or pay dues to keep their jobs, without ever being given the chance to vote on whether they wanted a union in the first place.

From a union's perspective, the Card Check path is great: There's no need to convince hearts and minds, just get 50 percent plus one worker to sign a card impulsively and you're well on your way. It's all good—except for that tricky part at the end. Because while unions can demand "automatic recognition," companies still have the right to say no to that demand and do what they feel is best for their employees and the company. And while many companies may give in at this point, feeling they have lost the battle, others do refuse and instead request a secret ballot election. Once the company refuses the demand for recognition, the campaign shifts back over to the first path - the NLRB schedules a secret ballot election, and the union is right back where they started.

Secret Ballot elections and Card Check, two paths that still carry risks for unions along with a cost. Estimates place the campaign cost to unions as much as $1,500 per worker, win or lose. Organizers would like to eliminate these risks and costs, which leads us to the third way a union can try to recruit new dues-paying members: Card Check with a Neutrality Agreement in place.

A Neutrality Agreement is an agreement between a union and an employer, in which the employer agrees to remain "neutral" during an organizing drive. Neutrality Agreements not only prevent the company from speaking out against a union, but they commonly require the company to give unions access to employee information, as well as access to the work premises for organizing purposes.

It may surprise you to hear that many companies consent to a Neutrality Agreement just to keep peace with unionized groups in other parts of the company. But even without an existing union presence, companies may agree to a Neutrality Agreement when unions apply pressure in other ways: through the media, through boycotts, by appealing to unionized vendors or customers. All of this is bad news for companies trying to remain competitive and union-free. These tactics are commonly known as corporate campaigns, and you'd be surprised how many unions are behind "consumer advocate" groups that are working to damage a company that wants to remain union-free.

A corporate campaign is a significant component of the union's organizing strategy. The goal is to generate sufficient pressure on a company, from the top down, to alter its assessment of the relative costs and benefits of yielding to the demands of the union. There are usually twenty-five to thirty union corporate campaigns going on in some form at any given time.

In theory, and often in practice, the reality of anti-corporate warfare, and many times the mere threat of it will make the company much more responsive to a union's demands. And that risk can lead to a Neutrality Agreement that includes a Card Check provision, which just means that the company agrees to automatically recognize the union if enough authorization cards are signed, no matter how long that process may take. This means that, except for collecting the signatures, the campaign is actually won before it even begins. According to the AFL-CIO, their success rate in such circumstances is a little more than 70 percent.

You can see where creating a union-proof workforce, well-educated on these tactics, can help you prevent unionization, even when the odds do not seem to be in your favor. Many a company has survived a Neutrality Agreement with a Card Check provision because the employees knew the risks and never signed enough cards for the union to take action.

Now, allow me to briefly deviate to address the fourth method by which a company can become unionized. I left it for last because it does not have anything to do with card-signing, Card Check, Neutrality Agreements, or corporate campaigns. A company can have a secret ballot election and win the election and then lose the election—all in the blink of an eye. How? It has to do with something called "Unfair Labor Practices."

If an employer wins the election, but along the way commits any Unfair Labor Practices (ULPs), the NLRB can order a new election, which will invalidate the original ballots. In extreme or unusual cases, the NLRB may even direct the employer to recognize the union immediately without another election. This situation is rare and typically is the result of a supervisor or an executive making out-of-control remarks or the company allowing situations that endanger the "laboratory conditions" required for NLRB elections. In a representation election, voting should occur in a "laboratory" environment, in which an experiment may be conducted, under conditions as close to ideal as possible, to determine the uninhibited desires of employees.

Secret ballot elections, Card Check campaigns, and Neutrality Agreements are three paths unions can take to becoming the workers' representative to management, and all depend on the use of union authorization cards or petitions, legally binding documents that your employees need to know about before a union ever knocks on their door.

That's why, to become union-proof, you need to take steps to educate your workforce about the value of their signatures and their e-signatures, and why those harmless-looking cards and petitions aren't nearly as harmless as the unions might lead them to believe.

In addition, to become union-proof and avoid the fourth path we have discussed, owners, executives, supervisors, and managers need to understand the rules surrounding union organizing campaigns, and how to avoid ULPs. I will review unfair labor practices at the end of this chapter.

Modern Labor Tactics

As an example, consider this a labor union representing Disney World character performers files an unfair labor practice charge protesting the alleged "chilling effect" of a company policy that forbids artists from publicly disclosing which characters they portray. Do you believe this scenario to be true or false?

We're going to take a look at modern labor tactics—which are more legislative than local, more online than off, and more political than you might think.

As "Mickey Mouse" as it sounds, the ULP scenario at Disney World is 100 percent real. The phrase "chilling effect" refers to Section 7 of the National Labor Relations Act, and the NLRB was referencing a policy in Disney's handbook.

Remember, Section 7 of the NLRA gives employees the right to engage in "concerted activities for the purpose of collective bargaining or other mutual aid or protection." Clearly, your employee handbook is the newest target of the NLRB. Any wording or restrictions that have a "chilling effect" on employees' Section 7 activity are going to be found unlawful—especially if the Board finds that employees would reasonably construe your rule or policy language to prohibit Section 7 activity.

The problem comes in deciding which words employees would view as prohibiting Section 7 activity. This question is every non-union employer's biggest challenge in this area.

Tied in closely with your employee handbooks is your social media policy. An emergency medical technician with American Medical Response was suspended after failing to document a customer complaint incident correctly. At home, she posted on

Facebook several derogatory remarks about her supervisor, calling him a "scumbag" and a "17"—an AMR's code for a psychiatric patient. AMR fires her.

Did the company violate Section 8A of the Act by terminating the employee for engaging in "protected activity" and by maintaining unlawful internet and blogging standards of conduct and solicitation policies? Yes, they did. Section 8A of the Act makes it a ULP for an employer to "interfere with, restrain, or coerce employees in the exercise of the rights guaranteed in Section 7" of the Act. The EMT and the company eventually reached a private settlement, but AMR was required by the Board to revise its social media policy nationwide. AMR agreed to change its rules regarding blogging, internet posting, standards of conduct, and solicitation and distribution, to prevent improper restriction of employees' rights both during and after working hours.

Let's look at one more social media policy case: A Lake Bluff, Illinois, BMW dealership published an employee handbook with a social media policy that included a section about "Courtesy." It read:

"Courtesy is the responsibility of every employee. Everyone is expected to be courteous, polite and friendly to our customers, vendors, and suppliers, as well as to their fellow employees. No one should be disrespectful or use profanity or any other language which injures the image or reputation of the Dealership."

Then, one of the dealership's salesmen, after attending a company-sponsored event, posted pictures and comments on Facebook relating to the inadequacy of the food at the event. That same day, he also posted pictures of an embarrassing incident at a Land Rover dealership—owned by the same company—that involved a salesperson and a customer's son. The BMW salesman was fired for his Facebook posts.

Did the company violate his Section 7 or 8 rights by firing him? Shockingly, the answer is no. The Board ultimately determined that the Facebook posts were an independent and unprotected cause for termination. He was not rehired, as there were no concerted activity violations. However, the Board did review the dealership's employee handbook and ordered it to be rewritten to prevent a "future" violation of the NLRA.

Now let's take a look at something that's traditionally not open to public view—company e-mail and the NLRB's "Purple Communications" decision. Purple Communications, Inc. maintained an electronic communications policy that prohibited employees from, among other things, using the company e-mail system to engage in "…activities on behalf of organizations or persons with no professional or business affiliation with the company…" or to send "…uninvited email of a personal nature."

Enter the Communication Workers of America, who attempted—and failed—to organize Purple Communications' employees. The CWA filed objections, along with ULPs alleging that the company's communication policy invalidated the election results and violated Section 8A of the NLRA.

Before you try to guess what happened, let me tell you how Purple Communications won the first round. An administrative law judge found the company's e-mail policy to be lawful, and dismissed both the CWA's objections and the ULPs based on a precedent: the case of "Register Guard." In the Register Guard case, the Board stated that the company's policy prohibiting employee use of the e-mail system for "non-job-related solicitations" did not violate Section 8A.

But in the Purple Communications case, the CWA didn't want to take no for an answer. Round two: With a different Board makeup and an appeal by the union, the Board reversed the Register Guard decision. They stated that employees with access to the company's e-mail system had an assumed right to use company e-mail during non-working time for "Section 7–protected communications" regarding terms and conditions of employment.

For now, the Purple Communications decision is limited to e-mail only and employees only, but it is only a matter of time before this ruling expands to other areas. Take, for example, this scenario: How can employers limit the use of e-mail when an employee sends an e-mail to other employees but cc's (carbon-copies) a non-employee, such as a union organizer...and then that organizer uses "Reply All" to respond?

The Purple Communication ruling came about via a reversal of a longstanding case precedent, and this overturning or precedent case law has become a standard method for the NLRB to change the rules of the game—generally not in favor of the employer.

Now, building off of our previous lesson about Card Check and Neutrality Agreements, let's take a look at other game-changing decisions by the NLRB.

Dana Corporation and the UAW entered into Card Check and Neutrality Agreements before any signatures on authorization cards were ever collected. However, the union did get enough signatures, and the UAW was recognized by the employer. But before a final contract was reached, the employees filed a decertification petition. The regional NLRB director dismissed their petition, calling it "inconsistent with the Board's "recognition bar" doctrine." The recognition bar states that after an employer voluntarily recognizes a union, neither an employee nor another union is allowed to file a new petition for a "reasonable period of time."

Dana employees continued the fight with the help of the National Right to Work Legal Defense Foundation, by requesting the Board to review the dismissal. The Board granted the request, saying that the issue was whether or not the Company's voluntary recognition of the union could keep employees from filing their decertification petition.

The Board eventually handed down their decision: Following a voluntary recognition, employees have forty-five days to file a petition to decertify the union. A rival union also has forty-five days to file an election petition. The petitions must be signed by at least 30 percent of bargaining unit employees. The employees must be notified of the voluntary recognition and their right to petition for a decertification or a representation election. If a petition is not filed within forty-five days, an election petition cannot be filed during the recognition bar period—"for a reasonable period of time."

Four years of cases later, that same ruling in the Dana case was overturned in an identical case with Lamons Gasket Company and the United Steelworkers. The parties entered into a Card Check Agreement. The company voluntarily recognized the USW as the sole representative of a unit of employees. Within forty-five days, the employees got 30 percent of the cards signed, and they filed for a decertification election. Then the Board overruled the Dana decision, returning to the previously established rule that following a voluntary recognition, an election period is barred for a "reasonable period of time." Only now, the Board defined that time as a period of at least six months, but not more than a year, after the first bargaining session between the employer and union.

You may have heard about Macy's and the Micro-Units decision. The NLRB determined that the UFCW-petitioned-for unit of forty-one cosmetics and fragrance employees at a Macy's retail store was appropriate. Macy's argued that the smallest appropriate unit must include either all employees at the location or at least all selling (sales) employees at the store.

The Board's decision was based on a case that again had overturned twenty years of precedent. The case was called Specialty Healthcare, and it involved the Steelworkers carving out a particular unit in the medical company to organize. The final decision was that when a union sought to represent a unit of employees "…who are readily identifiable as a group…and the Board finds that the employees in the group share a community of interest after considering the traditional criteria, the Board will find the petitioned-for unit to be an appropriate unit…"

If a company wants to present a case that a larger group should be considered, they must show that "…an overwhelming community of interest with the petitioned-for employees, such that there is no legitimate basis upon which to exclude individual employees from the larger unit because of the traditional community of interest factors overlap almost completely."

The Board found that Macy's failed to meet that burden, and the union was granted the win. The "Specialty Healthcare," or Micro-Unit rule, permits organizers to handpick and create units to create the best advantage. By crafting these smaller, micro-units, unions make it easier for them to win elections, because fewer people are needed to make up a majority vote. A win, especially in a retail environment, gives unions an organizing momentum.

Now, let's take a step back and review some of the traditional organizing tactics that unions have been utilizing for years, and touch on some of the modern updates to these tried-and-true methods.

There are many unions and organizers stuck in the traditional organizing mode. They love a good Xerox machine with colored paper, and a leafleting campaign, in which they pass out all manner of handouts. They utilize their local union hall—hangouts, coffee shops, and restaurants—to meet in small groups to recruit and start up campaigns. They will call employees at all hours of the day and night and begin making unannounced home visits to bring the entire family into the discussion. They will send letters to employees' homes and sometimes a video message via DVD or internet link.

Organizers will isolate employees who haven't signed a card, applying one-on- one pressure. Depending on the situation or the need, unions may involve outside parties to assist. These vocal "employee advocates" may include politicians, religious leaders, and sometimes even celebrities. Before we put a modern spin on these tactics, though, let's take a quick look at the NLRB's most recent gift to unions: The Expedited Election Rule.

The NLRB's Expedited Election Rule quickly became known as the "Ambush" Election Rule, because it dramatically shortened the campaign window from an average of thirty-eight days to as few as thirteen (averaging 23-24 days). This means that employees now have less time to research the union before voting, companies have less time to educate their workers, and the union doesn't have to sustain employee interest in the campaign for nearly as long.

Unions made sure that this rule included a provision requiring companies to release employees' personal information—including e-mail addresses and cell phone numbers. This last point is especially significant for today's modern organizing tactics because the rise of the Internet and social media has been a tremendous boon for union-organizing efforts.

In many cases, e-mail and text messages have taken the place of leaflets and posters, while social media has all but become the modern equivalent of the union meeting hall. Connected to this surge in electronic communication was yet another very union-friendly NLRB decision: The Board ruled that they would allow the use of electronic signatures for card signing. Employees may click SUBMIT on a web page rather than consider the implications over time and sign an authorization card in the presence or pressure of an organizer. If you combine Section 7 and Section 8 violations related to social media and company handbooks with micro-units, employees' use of e-mail, ambush elections, electronic signatures, and online organizing, and suddenly you've got the "perfect storm" of modern labor tactics.

By keeping union-organizing activities online and under the company's radar for as long as possible, companies are prevented from educating workers about the realities of union representation, and workers automatically become more vulnerable to a union sales pitch, because they're less likely to question what the union tells them. But these aren't the only "new tricks" left in labor's bag—although technically, this next trick isn't new at all; it's more of a reboot of an old tactic: the social justice campaign.

In the past, social justice campaigns allowed unions to paint themselves as champions of what's right and good, but in this new reboot, the unions, which create, orchestrate, and fund these so-called grassroots campaigns, stay hidden. In fact, many times, social justice campaign supporters don't even realize that a union is behind the effort. The "Fight for 15" social justice campaign is an excellent example of this. With a battle cry of raising the wage for fast-food and retail workers to $15 an hour, this effort is actually bankrolled by a major union, the SEIU, which directed the campaign not out of the goodness of their heart, but in the hopes of organizing low-wage retail and fast-food workers.

Another hidden-in-plain-sight tactic is the nonprofit community groups that call themselves "Worker Centers." These groups seem to be earnest, independent operations—"community groups" that are there to help workers—but the truth is, unions often provide the financial backing of worker centers. So why would unions go to all the trouble to hide behind these worker centers? Worker centers give unions a loophole that they can use to "sell the need" for a union to workers—without having to work under the legal restrictions that apply to union organizing.

"[Worker centers] aren't considered 'labor organizations' by law because they don't have continuing bargaining relationships with employers. That gives them more freedom in their use of picketing and other tactics than unions, which are constrained by national labor laws."

Do you see a pattern forming? Worker centers, social justice efforts, landmark legislative decisions, heavy political spending. Today's unions are thinking far outside the box to gain members, increase their revenues, and stay in business. Just like many other big businesses, unions are learning that to survive; they need to shift their strategies, embrace new technologies, and leverage their political power to meet their goals.

To stay union-proof, leaders like you need to educate your workers on the ways a union might try to manipulate them: directly through traditional means, or by pressuring the company, or by way of legal loopholes and political influence.

Signs of an Organizing Drive

Because your company is working to build a union-proof culture, employees already know that management is listening and acting in the company's best interests. Everyone understands that the company wishes to remain union-free and maintain a direct connection with its employees. But even with all of that in place, union organizing may still occur. A smart, proactive company can often detect the presence of organizing activity through simple observation of workplace dynamics.

It will always benefit unions to keep organizing activities quiet in a company for as long as possible—particularly with expedited or "ambush" elections taking place in only a few weeks. So for a union-proof company like yours, quickly identifying the signs of organizing activity can mean the difference between having the time to connect with and educate your employees or playing defense against union tactics.

Organizing activity can become evident in three different forms: physical, behavioral, and online.

I'll start with the most obvious: physical signs of organizing activity. Even today, hard-copy handouts are still in use by many unions—and if a campaign is in progress, you may find discarded flyers that cue you into this in the common areas of your workplace. In addition, if there are (paper) union authorization cards spotted, there's definitely organizing activity going on. For the time being, paper authorization cards are still the unions' most prevalent method of getting signatures from your employees. If anyone notices anti-company and/or pro-union graffiti in restrooms, break rooms, or other common areas, these signs aren't as "official" as a union document, but this kind of physical evidence is an indication that some level of union organization may be going on within the company. At the very least, there is employee unrest that needs to be addressed. You may notice news items being shared on bulletin boards or in flyers, such as articles about union settlements in your industry or city. And finally, if you see union wearables, like buttons or T-shirts, that's a sure sign that organizing is underway. Often, these sorts of physical displays are a test of whether or not the management will attempt to interfere with the employees' Section 7 and 8 rights. For the union, the company's reaction may be a way to gauge the temperature of the campaign.

Now, while physical evidence can confirm suspicions of union activity, actual early awareness requires your leaders to be connected to—and really know—your employees. This is where behavioral evidence comes into play.

The way your employees act—toward their managers and each other—can speak volumes about a union-organizing drive, and what's going on inside their heads. Let's look at some examples.

In the early stages of organizing activity, there is lots of conversation, debate, questions, and interest by the employees. You may notice the following: small groups of employees gathering in unusual places; groups that may include employees who might not typically socialize with one another, with the tone of their discussions more serious than usual. You may even see upticks in heated discussions between employees. However intense the discussions may become, these groups will often dissolve quickly when a member of management approaches. As a campaign progresses, employees may change their usual routines, taking lunch or breaks at different times than they have in the past, and you might see diverse groups of employees gathering, and employees who may or may not even work together spending more time together.

Another sign of organizing is the noticeable presence of strangers or even discharged employees. Customers or delivery people may linger longer than usual, as workers strike up conversations. Be aware of any employee or outsider "casually" collecting employee names and contact information, or copying or taking pictures of any posted employee lists.

New employee alliances may form, and new leaders may emerge—or formerly popular employees may, seemingly without cause, somehow lose favor with their coworkers. Complaints may now be made by a delegation, rather than a single employee raising a concern.

You might notice employees spending more time on their phones, texting or accessing social media while at work. When this happens, it's often because employees are sharing information with one another, and because everyone wants to be "in the know" as quickly as possible.

Further into the campaign, as things become more specific, employees may begin demonstrating an unusual interest in company policy, employee handbooks, or benefit plans. Similarly, their language may change, and they may even become argumentative in group meetings as they ask about improving working conditions or wages and benefits. Employees may develop "corporate-speak or "legal phrases" as they repeat union information.

There may be increased complaints from employees, and some may begin using union buzzwords like "grievance," "arbitration," or "security." As a part of their organizing strategy, union organizers have to generate dissatisfaction among employees, so negative talk and complaints often increase as these ideas take root.

Later in the campaign, if they disagree with their coworkers, individuals may act out of character. If these kinds of divisions occur, formerly happy people may suddenly become sullen and incommunicative, and absenteeism may even increase. Employees who were previously friendly to management may stop talking to their supervisors; this is sometimes out of fear of accidentally talking about the campaign, or sometimes they only feel awkward about the union activity and just prefer to stay quiet. At its most extreme, this warning sign can mean that some employees may even uncharacteristically try to provoke or irritate their supervisors.

Another behavioral change you may notice is that a recently hired employee may actually be a union "salt," who begins to organize employees openly. These "salts" apply to work for the company for the sole purpose of organizing for a union, and they may also "act up" in the hopes of being fired and subsequently filing an Unfair Labor Practice charge against the company, further strengthening the union's organizing position.

Finally, your HR department may notice a significant change in the rate of employee turnover—either in an upward or a downward direction. Similarly, if your HR department conducts regular exit interviews, you may notice a trend of employees leaving to "escape an unpleasant environment," as union organizing changes the tone of your work culture.

Of course, none of these warning signs by themselves is proof of union activity—but neither should they be ignored. Similarly, any *single* sign I've described here doesn't necessarily mean there's union activity, either, but the more employees who exhibit these behaviors or, the more times you encounter such physical evidence, the more likely it is that an organizing campaign has taken root.

Finally, the signs of organizing activity *can* be both physical and behavioral, but *online* activity can be just as telling. Unions have become incredibly savvy online, and they know how to bring employees together through social media and websites. Having an online community of like-minded individuals is compelling for employees, and it can certainly make employees feel as though everyone is jumping on the union bandwagon. One of the first signs of union organization can be on social media, as platforms like Facebook make it very simple to set up private groups and communicate quickly and easily between the union and your employees.

Make sure that as a company, you have a practice of *not* spying on your employees, but you should regularly check in on social media, an activity I like to call "social listening." This means setting up saved searches for any time the company name is mentioned. It also means knowing your employees and what's important to them, understanding where their "virtual watercoolers" may be.

More sophisticated unions—or more advanced campaigns, about which you may already be aware—can and do make use of full-blown websites. These sites usually have one or two objectives—and sometimes both! First, the site may seek to damage the company in the style of a corporate campaign, calling its integrity, business practices, or treatment of employees into question. Or second, the site may be overtly working to organize employees, and it may publicly air grievances, state demands, or offer an online authorization card (A-card) for employees to print and sign or electronically sign and submit.

Finally, online campaigns may make use of e-mail, Twitter accounts, RSS feeds, other social media apps, and more to directly deliver information about the union to employees' in-boxes, tablets, and phones. It's important that your leadership team knows what these signs are, and what to do if they seem to be having an influential effect on employees.

Union-proof companies make a point to train and educate supervisors and managers to be alert, as they are often the closest to employees and are most in tune with any subtle behavioral changes. As a union-proof company, you need to create a precise method for your front-line leaders to notify upper management if they suspect that any organizing activity is taking place. Supervisors as your real first line of defense need to be trained to handle these situations. I will cover two methods TIPS and FOE right after this next section.

Representation: The Legal Process

For the first fifty-plus years of the NLRB's existence, the average petition-to-election time was thirty-eight days, but that all changed with the introduction of the Expedited Election rule. Also known as the Ambush Election rule, the petition-to-election time frame can now be anywhere from thirteen to twenty-four days.

This shortened time frame has eliminated much of a union-proof company's time to educate their employees about the upcoming election, giving the Union an advantage. The current election process under the NLRA begins when employees, the employer, or a union e-files an election petition with the NLRB to determine whether the union is entitled to represent a group of employees for the purposes of collective bargaining.

To file a petition, a union must first demonstrate to the NLRB a "showing of interest…" which means a minimum of 30 percent of employees in a group appropriate for collective bargaining indicates a desire to be represented by the union. The official "showing of interest" comes in the form of signatures on a union authorization card, either digital or actual, or they can be on a union petition.

The Petition for Election is then filed with the NLRB Regional Office that has geographic jurisdiction over the specific location involved.

It's important to note that there are actually three types of election petitions, each with a different purpose. The first type of petition, the RC petition, or Certification of Representative petition, is typically filed by a union and is the most common petition used in secret ballot representation elections.

Before the NLRB can approve an RC petition for election, two things have to take place: First, there must be a showing of interest of least 30 percent by submission of signed and dated union authorization cards. Unions then have forty-eight hours after filing to present this physical evidence of interest. Second, the employer must refuse to recognize the union, which occurs when the union demands recognition.

The second type of petition may be filed by an employer and is known as a Representation Matters, or RM, Petition. The company can file this sort of petition without any showing of interest. The company must allege and prove that the union has demanded recognition. That demand could be in the form of a union's submission of a proposed contract or a request for a contract; picketing for recognition or organization; or a request for contract renewal by an incumbent union. This final point means that a company can file an RM petition to show that a currently represented union no longer has the support of a majority of the employees.

The third type of petition is filed by employees who no longer desire union representation and file a Decertification of Representative or RD petition. This petition requires the same 30 percent showing of interest from employees as the RC petition a union files. The employer cannot instigate or assist employees. They can, however, advise employees as to the proper procedure for filing the petition, if asked.

Now, together let's walk through the process of what happens after an RC petition is e-filed. First, both the NLRB *and* the union must notify the company, electronically. The employer then receives a detailed description of the NLRB's representation case procedures, along with the date of the pre-election hearing and required paperwork called a "statement of position" form. This form helps the company identify the issues they might want to raise at the pre-election hearing.

Once the employer is notified, the election clock is running with virtually no way to stop it. At this point, it is imperative that the company implement a communication strategy immediately. Employees need to hear all sides of the issue to make an informed decision.

The employer must now pay particular attention to all due dates, and filing and posting requirements, right down to the time of day when many items are required. A missed deadline or posting could cost the company ULPs—or worse—the election.

In-house counsel or outside attorneys can assist with all of these steps and more—it's a good idea for a union-proof company to have already assembled this team, long before a petition is filed.

As soon as the company is notified of the petition, it's legally required to post the Notification of Petition. The purpose of this posting is to let employees know about the campaign and how the campaign is to be conducted. Notices are posted wherever the company usually posts employee communications, and it should also be posted electronically if that is one of the company methods. This posting might seem like a minor step, but if these notices aren't posted within forty-eight hours—and kept up for the duration of the campaign—the union could turn the company's "failure to post" into an opportunity to have the election overturned.

Unless there are complex issues at play, a Pre- Election Hearing is scheduled precisely eight days after the petition has been filed. The NLRB holds this hearing to confirm that the union is seeking an "appropriate" bargaining unit—and they determine this through their "community-of-interests" test. This test assesses whether or not the employees have "substantial similar interests in wages, hours, and working conditions."

No later than the day before this hearing, the company must file their Statement of Position form. As part of their Statement of Position, companies are required to compile and provide to the NLRB and the union a basic list of all prospective voters: their full names; their job classifications; what shifts they work; and their work locations. Contact information isn't included here—that comes later.

The Statement of Position is the company's one-and-only chance to add or remove individual employees from eligibility to vote. If a company fails to compile this list of employees in advance of the hearing, they agree to the group as the union defines it. This is also the only time to exclude anyone whom the company identifies as a supervisor from the voting unit. If this is not done in the pre-election hearing, the bargaining unit stands, and the employees in question won't be resolved until after the election takes place. The critical point of defining the supervisor goes beyond being a part of the voting unit. Clearly identifying supervisors determines whether or not an employer can lawfully use that person as a company spokesperson during the campaign.

The outcome of the NLRB's pre-election hearing includes setting a date for a secret ballot election. At this point, the company will receive the time, place and method the union would like for the actual employee vote.

At this stage, the company has forty-eight hours to compile a Voter's List with contact information for all of the employees in the voting unit, including phone numbers and e-mail addresses. Three working days before the election date, employers must also post a Notice of Election, providing all eligible employees the information they need about the election and the voting process. Just as with the Notice of Petition, this must be posted electronically, as well, if that's how the company usually communicates. During a campaign, the union has the right to try to organize workers—which they will do, especially now that they have the Voter's List information. The union is given ten days to use that list, but depending on the percentage of cards already signed, a union can choose to waive all or some of that time, in order to speed the election along. Both the union and the company can communicate with employees, until and up to twenty-four hours before the vote.

Now, let's talk a little bit about election day. RC elections are decided by a majority of votes cast. The company wins with a majority of "no" votes, and the union wins with a majority of "yes" votes. A tie goes to the company.

On the day of the election, the NLRB offers both the union and the company the opportunity to designate an equal number of observers. These monitors help to identify voters and count ballots. During the voting process, managers and supervisors must stay away from the area in which the election is being conducted, avoiding any appearance of campaigning. Upon arrival at the voting place, employee-voters proceed to the Board agent and identify themselves by stating their name. The officer hands a ballot to each eligible voter. They do not sign the ballot. A ballot with any identifying marks is considered void.

A single question is printed on the ballot: "Do you wish to be represented for purposes of collective bargaining by the union?" There are two squares, one marked "yes" and one marked "no." Voters enter the voting booth and mark their ballot in secret. They then fold the ballot before leaving the voting booth, and they deposit it in a ballot box that is supervised by the Board agent. Then they leave the polling area.

Any observer or Board agent may challenge any voter as ineligible. That person is still allowed to vote, via a challenged ballot. The actual voter eligibility will be resolved later, if necessary. Note - the contested votes are not opened unless the outcome of the election might be affected by those ballots.

Under Expedited Election rules, after the election, any objections or ULPs from either party must be filed within seven days of the vote count. The results may even be set aside if the Board determines that conduct by either party has created an atmosphere that interfered with an employees' freedom of choice. In the event of a loss, the union must wait a full year from the date of the election before another election can be held.

The union-organizing campaign, the petition for election, and the election procedure are all legal processes, which means that all parties involved must go into the actions with a thorough understanding of the law—or suffer the consequences. Because you are committed to making your workplace union-proof, it would serve you to understand these processes and the part you should play in keeping the proceedings legal as well as keeping your workforce union-free.

What Not to Say: T.I.P.S.

Continuing to work during a union campaign is stressful for everyone involved—employees are being pressured by union organizers to sign cards and by their coworkers to choose a side. Senior management is focused on strategy and the "what-ifs" involved if the campaign proceeds to an election. As for your first line of defense, the managers and supervisors are right there in the thick of it, working to help the company build a union-proof culture while still trying to keep everyone focused on the job at hand.

To make matters even worse, during a union-organizing drive or election, your managers must actively remain aware of what they can or cannot say and do, or face possible legal consequences—in the form of an Unfair Labor Practice, or ULP. If during a union election campaign, any employee feels that their Section 7 rights have been violated, they may file a ULP against the company with the National Labor Relations Board. A union may also file a ULP, or they may wait until the election is held, and if they lose, then they may file an objection to the election at that time.

If a ULP or complaint against your company is upheld, and it is deemed to have affected the outcome of the election, the consequences can be severe. An election can be "set aside" and another vote may be scheduled. In that case, a union that may have lost in a landslide suddenly has another chance to win. Or worse, elections can be awarded directly to the union without there even being another election—if the violations are severe enough.

ULPs of this nature can be devastating to a company that has been working to be union-proof. It is all of management's responsibility—from the CEO to the front-line supervisor—to avoid these kinds of ULPs. As I've stated previously, Section 7 guarantees employees the "right to self-organization, to form, join, or assist labor organizations, to bargain collectively through representatives of their own choosing, and to engage in other concerted activities for the purpose of collective bargaining or other mutual aid or protection," as well as the right to "refrain from any or all such activities."

This means that employees are free to choose—and that freedom is ensured against interference by Section 8. Section 8 makes it an unfair labor practice for employers or unions to stand in the way of employees as they exercise the rights guaranteed in Section 7 of the NLRA.

During a campaign, ULPs are something with which companies don't want to take any chances. The good news is that once managers know the rules, they can develop the skills to avoid certain behaviors and learn to communicate with employees "correctly" during an organizing campaign. It's also a skill that improves with practice.

There's a handy acronym to help remind managers of the things that can and cannot be said or done during this time. In fact, most of the common ULPs can be avoided by following what's known as the "T.I.P.S." rule—with each letter signifying a type of conduct that should be prevented during a union campaign.

- Threaten
- Interrogate
- Promise
- Spy

We'll explore these four elements of the T.I.P.S. rule by examining real-world examples in which managers, albeit sometimes unintentionally, put their companies at risk for ULPs.

A manager for Mississippi Chemical once told employees: "…all the union would do was to knock employees down to a minimum wage, take all their benefits, and then they would have to bargain from scratch." The board ruled that this statement was, in fact, an Unfair Labor Practice, and the punishment, if you will, was a cease-and-desist order, NLRB postings, and more.

This statement violated the "T" in the T.I.P.S. rule, which stands for *THREATEN*. During a union campaign, no member of the supervisory staff is permitted to threaten employees in any way if they should choose to support a union. For example, you cannot threaten employees with the loss of jobs or benefits, company discrimination, or retaliation if they vote in favor of the union. The threat of retaliation is as bad as actually punishing an employee for union activity; both can draw a ULP.

In a federal judge ruling, several bus drivers for the Latino Express were seen by managers leaving a restaurant with some union organizers. In the days that followed, drivers who were seen at the restaurant were asked to meet with managers about union support—and two of those employees were even fired.

The Board ruled that this action constituted an Unfair Labor Practice, and the employer was ordered to rehire the drivers. This situation violated the "I" in the T.I.P.S. rule, which stands for *INTERROGATION*. Supervisors are not permitted to interrogate employees about their feelings on unions, or about any union activity. They cannot ask even their most trusted employees whom they support; who else is supporting the union; why people are signing cards; or what the union is telling people. However, if employees ask any questions about the union, supervisors can answer them, but they cannot, in turn, ask the employees any questions regarding union activity or their part in it. Asking an employee how he or she feels about union promises is considered interrogation.

The Newburg Egg Company representatives once promised: "...future benefits if employees voted against the union and told employees a vote for the union would be futile..." The Board ruling on this statement? They determined it was an Unfair Labor Practice and ordered a third election. In the first election, the union lost 43–80. The union lost the second election 41–77. In the third election, the union lost 52–62. This was out of 170 eligible voters, so there were fifty-six employees who did not vote, and with a ten-vote swing, you can see what a ULP *almost* cost the Newburg Egg Company.

The ULP came because company management promised benefits in exchange for votes. Under the T.I.P.S. Rule, the "P" stands for *PROMISE*. Managers cannot promise any workers that wages, benefits or working conditions will improve if the union is kept out. To expand on this "promises" concept, managers may not promise that wage increases, longer vacations, or more benefits will be theirs if they stop signing cards. Supervisors may not promise favored treatment or promotions to employees who help keep the union out. Quite simply, it is best to not make *any* promises to *any* employee during a union campaign.

DHL Express guards once engaged "...in unlawful surveillance by standing among or near hand billers while police investigated the presence of nonemployee union agents on the edge of the employer's property." The board ruling was an Unfair Labor

Practice, and then the Board set aside the election results—Did the DHL win? Did the union win? —No one knows and a second election was ordered.

Under the T.I.P.S. Rule, the "S" stands for *SPY*. Managers or representatives of management are not permitted to spy on employees in any attempt to get information about the union. Any surveillance of employees or union representatives is strictly prohibited. Even the *appearance* of monitoring, such as wandering around the parking lot jotting things down in a notebook or eavesdropping on private conversations, could be taken the wrong way and reported to the Board. A manager telling employees that they know who is supporting the union could be considered a threat or evidence that they have been spying. The managers of Latino Express were actually spying on their employees at the restaurant before they *interrogated* them.

T.I.P.S. involves the prohibition of these activities: Threatening, Interrogating, Promising, or Spying. So, how can supervisors and managers discuss the negative aspects of unionization without invoking the "T" for *Threaten*? How do managers get the vital information about employee concerns and union-generated issues out to their workers without invoking the "I" for *Interrogate*? How can managers deliver a positive message to employees without invoking the "P" for *Promise*? And how can managers assess the strength of the union's support without invoking the "S" for *Spy*?

There is a way, and it's called F.O.E.—for Facts, Opinions, and Experience, and I will talk about it next.

One thing I like about the T.I.P.S. rule is that it's very cut-and-dried—you follow the rule, and you will avoid a potential legal entanglement for yourself and your company. Campaigns are stressful enough. Have your managers and supervisors commit T.I.P.S. to memory, and they will know exactly what kind of communication should be avoided during an organizing campaign.

What to Say: F.O.E.

When you're union-proof, a union campaign isn't something to be feared—it's something to be managed. You've already learned that one of the best ways to avoid Unfair Labor Practices is by knowing what *not* to say during an organizing drive. The T.I.P.S. rules - do not Threaten, Interrogate, Promise, or Spy.

So, what can you say? You can use the acronym, F.O.E., to help you remember three important rules. F.O.E. stands for *Facts, Opinions,* and *Experiences.* You have to understand that the way your managers communicate with employees can be your greatest asset in remaining union-free—or it can a potential source of trouble during a campaign. In fact, some employers can become so confused or concerned about what can legally be said to employees regarding unions that they often actually train supervisors and managers to say nothing at all!

This is a problem, because while having supervisors "say nothing" may seem like a safe strategy to avoid ULPs, their silence does nothing to *counter* union claims or advance the company's position to remain union-free in any way. There's no quicker path to unionization than a management team that looks like it doesn't care enough to address employees concerns!

Section 8 of the NLRA protects workers' rights by leaving them free to choose whether or not they wish to be represented by a union. While there are rules keeping both unions and employers from any coercion of employees, there are many more limitations on what an employer is allowed to say than what a union can say.

For instance, the T.I.P.S. rules do not apply to unions. A union, with few exceptions, *can* legally make promises to employees. The NLRB has frequently held that union promises about improving wages, benefits, and working conditions would *not* unfairly influence employees to vote *for* the union, because "employees are generally able to understand that a union cannot obtain benefits automatically by winning an election...."

In other words, it's assumed that employees already know that only the employer has the power to keep its promises and that a union's pledges are not guarantees. But that's not always the case. This ruling assumes that all employees understand how unions work—or, barring that, it assumes that unions will at least be honest in educating workers about the pros and cons of union representation. That's a very naïve assumption when you consider that a sizeable percentage of dues money is often at stake, not to mention the struggle to maintain membership numbers.

This is why empowering your supervisors on how to communicate during a campaign is so important—because the worst thing a manager can do during a union campaign is…nothing. When "lack of knowledge" paralyzes those front-line supervisors, employees are cheated out of their manager's participation, their education, and their honest communication…the most powerful assets your company has to remain union-free. But what should be said to employees—and how?

For the most part, conversations about labor unions should be casual conversations, to be handled in the same way you talk about other company issues. Utilize T.I.P.S. Rules training to avoid danger spots, and then focus on the sorts of things about which you *can* talk. That's where the F.O.E. Rules come into play. With F.O.E., the "F" stands for *FACTS*. Supervisors and managers are always encouraged to share the facts about unions with employees. This could include the sharing of information, such as labor statistics, as well as discussions about the fact that employees could actually lose some benefits during contract negotiations with a union and that union promises are not guarantees.

Here are a few examples of factual statements that managers *can* share with employees without fear of any violations. Just stick to the "F" in F.O.E. for *FACTS*. "Unions represent less than 7 percent of the private sector workforce today." Of course, make sure you have the most up-to-date percentage here for accuracy!

Here's another: "The unions' main source of income is member dues."

Or, "Did you know that in collective bargaining, a union can guarantee nothing?"

Or, "Employees might find that their wages and benefits have gone up, stayed the same, or even been cut after negotiations are complete."

Or, "Just because an employee signed a union authorization card does not mean they have to vote for the union in an election because the election will be via a secret ballot."

These are all good examples of Facts: transparent, verifiable, not threatening in any way—and completely legal!

"O" stands for *OPINIONS*. Managers are always allowed to share their personal views about union representation, including their opinion on whether or not a union is needed at their location. Let's try on some of these opinions and see how this type of dialogue might work with employees.

"I feel a union could cause a loss of personal communication due to union members having to go through a union steward."

"Employees already receive competitive wages and benefits without having to pay someone else to represent them."

"I don't think a union would be good for employees. That's just my opinion."

Next, "E" is for *EXPERIENCES*. If a supervisor or manager has ever had any personal experience with a union, they should always feel free to share those experiences with their employees. This does not necessarily mean that they personally were a member of a union, but perhaps they grew up with family members or friends who were in a union and thus experienced life events through that association with those people.

Experiences are just that—things that managers or supervisors have personally experienced or observed. If the supervisor belonged to a union in a previous job, they could relate how it impacted their company, altered their job, or changed that workplace. The supervisor can point out experiences that he or she may have had with someone they knew who was getting less in a contract after unionization than they had before.

Supervisors can discuss the fact that unions do go on strike, and they may give an example of how a strike played out for someone they knew, causing stress, lost wages, family hardships, and more. And finally, supervisors can show experiences through articles or online stories about union layoffs, concessions, strikes, or corruption. The internet is a treasure trove of experiences, just waiting to be shared!

All supervisors or managers involved in a union campaign can share any facts they know about unions, their personal opinions on why a union wouldn't be a good idea or any experiences they or others they know have had regarding unions. They just need to remember the F.O.E. rules. Together, T.I.P.S. and F.O.E. will make sure the managers and your company stay clear of ULP charges. In fact, by taking the time to communicate with employees, managers can connect with their teams, answer questions, and correct misinformation. These are the things that win elections for companies. These are the things that make companies union-proof.

Unfair Labor Practice Charges

It should be clear by now that making your organization union-proof involves a basic understanding of labor law, making sure your team plays by the rules, and being able to recognize when your opponent doesn't. Let's take a look at what happens when an employer or a union breaks the rules—resulting in an Unfair Labor Practice charge.

When you hear about a ULP, the typical response is, "What has the company done now?" But employees, employers, and even labor organizations themselves file tens of thousands of charges each year against unions and union officials. Union members even may file ULPs against their own union because the union failed to represent its members fairly. Employees file ULPs against union leaders for intimidation, coercion, violence, and many other labor law violations. So, what exactly ARE ULPs?

The National Labor Relations Act keeps employers from standing in the way of employees' right to "organize, form, join, or assist a labor organization" (known as Section 7 rights). That interference includes collective bargaining, as well as employees, working together to improve terms and conditions of employment. It also protects those same employees' right to refrain from any such activity.

Labor organizations have to follow these same rules and respect the employees' right to organize—or to remain union-free—and if they don't, ULPs are filed.

There are five categories of ULPs defined in the Act that apply to all employers. These five categories cover everything you need to be aware of to *avoid* charges of a ULP. The first is *interference, restraint, or coercion*. Most violations of this section involve supervisors who threaten employees, who question employees who assert their labor rights, or who make false statements to workers seeking unionization.

The second thing that can get you into trouble is *employer domination or support of a labor organization*. Employers may not interfere with the formation or administration of any labor organization, neither may they contribute financially or with any other support to such an organization. You can see how that could create a conflict of interest!

Third, there's the danger of *discrimination on the basis of labor activity*. Companies may not discriminate against any employee in hiring, in tenure of employment, or in any other term or condition of employment to encourage or discourage membership in any labor organization.

Fourth, employers must take care not to discharge or otherwise discriminate against an employee in any terms or conditions of employment in *retaliation for going to the NLRB*. Employees cannot be discriminated against because of charges filed or testimony given.

Finally, the fifth category of ULPs applies to unionized companies, and that's *a refusal to bargain*. If a company refuses to bargain with its employees' representatives, if it imposes conditions on its willingness to bargain, or if it refuses to recognize a majority union, ULPs can be filed. Similarly, if a unionized employer takes unilateral actions, or refuses to provide necessary information to union representatives, that is seen as a *lack of participation in the bargaining process.* If an employer refuses to sign a written contract once an agreement is reached, that's a clear violation of the Act, and grounds for a ULP charge.

So there are the five categories applicable to employers. Now, what does the NLRA prohibit unions from doing?

Let's review some examples of several actual Section 8 ULP charges that have been filed against unions with the NLRB:

- Restraining or coercing employees regarding their right not to support a union, or restraining or coercing an employer in its choice of a bargaining representative.
- Causing or trying to cause an employer to discriminate against an employee for the purpose of encouraging or discouraging union membership.
- Refusing to engage in good-faith collective bargaining.
- Engaging in strikes, boycotts, or other coercive actions for illegal purposes.
- Charging membership fees that are excessive or discriminatory.
- Getting (or trying to get) an employer to side with the union.
- Getting (or trying to get) a company to agree to pay for work that is not performed. This is called "featherbedding."
- Picketing for recognition for over thirty days without petitioning the NLRB for an election
- Entering into a "hot cargo" agreement. (This prohibits the employer from doing business with any vendor or supplier not affiliated with the union.)
- Striking or picketing a health-care establishment without giving the required notice.

Let's go back to the fact that twenty to thirty *thousand* ULPs are filed each year. The truth is, they can be filed by an employer, an employee, or a union that feels that a violation has occurred. The National Labor Relations Board reports that these charges are usually filed within six months of the unfair labor practice occurrence itself.

The NLRB's General Counsel is charged with investigating all of these ULPs every year, and it has the final authority on whether or not a complaint is to be considered valid. To ease up on that workload, the initial investigation of the complaint is delegated to the NLRB's Regional Director, in the location wherever the charge has been filed. Board agents gather evidence, including affidavits from parties and witnesses. The party that filed the ULP is responsible for bringing its own witnesses to support their charge. If they aren't able to do this, then the charge is typically dismissed.

The regional director will review the agents' findings, and then make a decision within thirty days as to whether or not to proceed with the charge. Before that decision, it's entirely possible that the charges may be settled by the involved parties, or it could be withdrawn or even just dismissed by the Regional Director. More than ten to fifteen thousand of filed ULPs each year are withdrawn or dismissed. If a filer is unhappy with the Regional Director's decision to dismiss a charge, however, they can appeal to the General Counsel. If the General Counsel agrees with the decision to dismiss the charge, that's it; the decision is final.

However, if the Regional Director finds that there is merit to the charge, a formal complaint is then filed, spelling out the violations of the NLRA. In most of these cases, in which the board agents have found probable merit, the parties can reach a settlement. But if no settlement can be reached, a formal complaint is issued, which leads to an administrative law judge of the NLRB conducting a hearing. Typically, a decision is made about the merits of a charge within seven to twelve weeks, although some cases do take much longer.

Keep in mind throughout this whole process that if an employee is the one who filed the charges, that employee is protected against retaliation from either the union or the employer. So, you might be wondering at this point, how are cases like these ultimately resolved? Under its statutes, the NLRB doesn't have the authority to impose traditional penalties or punitive damages on the employer or the union, but it does have the power to provide "whole relief." That means they can order the union or the employer to "cease and desist" in their unfair labor practice and then remedy the violation. If an individual employee is injured by a ULP that was committed by an employer, the Board may order the employer to compensate the employee, and that compensation may come in the form of reinstatement, payment of lost wages and benefits, or seniority credits. The Board regularly orders parties guilty of ULPs to post a notice informing the workers of the Board's decision.

In the more severe cases, the NLRB's General Counsel may involve the federal courts for an injunction. Use of this power is rare, but its purpose is to preserve the employer's current status while waiting for Board's decision or to prevent employees from suffering irreparable harm. It's important to note that if the employer fails to comply with an NLRB order, the Board has the authority to find the employer to be in "contempt of court" and impose civil and/or criminal penalties on that employer. These kinds of contempt penalties include fines against the employer as well as personal fines and even jail time for individual supervisors and managers.

Actual fines, actual jail time—clearly, a ULP is something you'll want to avoid at all costs. Now that you know what's at stake make sure your managers and leaders are educated on T.I.P.S. and F.O.E., so that you are confident they know what they can and cannot say before, during, and after union campaigns.

Chapter 5

Life with a Union

Collective Bargaining

Sometimes it helps to consider "worst case scenario" situations. That's what this "Life with a Union" chapter is all about - helping you plan for the worst, while at the same time, helping you create an environment- and culture – where unions simply aren't necessary. Because when a union becomes "certified" to be your employees' "bargaining representative," the next step is "Collective Bargaining... a slippery slope where employees could end up with more than what they have, about the same, or they COULD end up with less!

I've covered what happens during an organizing campaign – but I haven't spent any time talking about the aftermath. What happens if, when the campaign ends, when the votes are counted and maybe even after the appeals are done, you find out that the union has actually... won?

That's the nightmare scenario, your life with a union. Before you'd even be able to process the loss, though, you'd have to get right back up, circle your wagons and get ready for the next stage: collective bargaining.

The term "collective bargaining" was first used in 1891 by Beatrice Webb, a founder of the field of industrial relations in Britain. Webb was a sociologist, labor historian, and a social reformer, but she was first and foremost an economist, and one of the founders of the London School of Economics. Together with her husband Sidney, she authored the book, "Industrial Democracy" in 1897, in which they introduced the concept of collective bargaining as an economic model - used exclusively by unions.

Beatrice Webb: "In non-union environments, employees, applying for a job, accept or refuse the terms offered by the employer with communication with his fellow associates and without any consideration other than his or her circumstances of his positions and thus makes an "individual bargain." But if a group of employees, organized into a unit, become unionized, and send a representative to negotiate on behalf of the unit, then the dynamic immediately changes. Instead of an employer making a series of separate contracts with isolated individuals, he meets with the collective will, and settles, in a single contract, the principles upon which, for a set period, all employees of a particular group, class or grade, will be engaged."

Let's start by defining what a *union contract* is. A labor union contract is an agreement between a labor union and an employer, spelling out the conditions and terms of employment for workers, as well as the obligations and responsibilities of the employer. The contract governs wages, benefits, and working conditions for all of the employees in the particular bargaining unit.

If you think that sounds like a fairly powerful document, you'd be right. It's one of the reasons so many employees vote for a union, based on the promises the union gives to them—to get that contract—but what many employees don't realize is that contracts, and the promises that unions make, aren't automatic.

It makes sense when you think about it. A contract is a document that contains an agreement between two different sides—but, as you might imagine, a company and a union might not immediately see eye to eye on every issue. In fact, they might not ever see eye to eye on some of the union's requests.

How can the company and the union get from where they are after the election, to the point where they are in complete agreement on everything that is to be included in the contract? It is as Beatrice Webb described: through the process of *collective bargaining*. In collective bargaining, both parties—the employer and the union—come together through a series of meetings to craft a union contract to which both parties can agree.

During collective bargaining, the union, and the company must follow certain rules as they try to hammer out a new deal. And those rules are spelled out in the National Labor Relations Act. The NLRA states that the company and the union both must bargain in good faith, meaning that they do have to *try* to find some common ground. But the National Labor Relations Act also states very clearly that the obligation to bargain in good faith "does not compel either party to agree to a proposal or require the making of a concession."

That statement means that if the union asks for something, the company does have the right to say "no" if it *genuinely* feels the request is not in the best interests of the company or its employees. The thing to realize about collective bargaining is that the decisions made during these meetings are made by people. Some are on the union side, and some are on the company side—but they are all people nonetheless. And people have opinions, attitudes, strong points, and even flaws.

On one side of the table, the company will have some of its executives and more than likely its lawyers present. On the other side, the union could have any number of people present—from employee representatives to local business agents to officials from the international union headquarters. Many times union negotiators are even flown in just to handle the bargaining sessions, agents who've never even met the people—the employees—they're supposed to be representing.

As for the union people who do know the employees, the organizers who have worked to get the union voted in, well, like any other salesperson, they may move on to their next organizing target and leave others from the union to "close the deal." This can be quite a shock to the employees who have placed their trust in those organizers to bargain for everything they had promised.

This is called "bargaining" because both parties approach the table with their objectives. There are things the company wants, things the union wants, and things the employees want, as well. The only leverage that the unions have to get what they want comes in the form of the wages, benefits, and working conditions that the employees currently have. In collective bargaining, everything goes on the table—wages, benefits, vacation time, and holiday pay—it's all up for negotiation. Often unions will use these very benefits to negotiate for clauses that the unions want in a contract, but that don't necessarily help their new members.

These provisions may include the Dues Check-Off Clause, which allows the union to take authorized dues deductions *directly* from an employee's paycheck, just like taxes are deducted. Another clause might be the Super Seniority Clause, which creates an exclusive union "inner circle" of employees who are the last to go and the first to come back during a time of layoffs or recalls... And in Non-Right-to-Work states, it is legal for the union to negotiate a Union Security Clause, which states that every employee must pay the union dues or a fee as a "condition of employment." In other words, they either pay—or the union will have them fired.

However, unions aren't the only ones who know what they want from a union contract—companies do, too. That's why, in just about every contract negotiated with a union today, you'll find something called a Management Rights Clause, which makes sure that, with or without a union, management will still continue to make the day-to-day decisions about how to run the company. Unions like to talk about the power that they can bring to a workplace—but standard contract clauses like those involving management rights make sure that the real power in a unionized company stays with management.

In many ways, collective bargaining is the place where union promises are confronted by the reality of the business. It's a game of give-and-take, and it's a game with risks—particularly for employees. So, bargaining begins from the bottom, with everything on the table, and that's how employees can actually end up with less at the end of the negotiations than what they had at the beginning. What's more, while collective bargaining is underway, wages are frozen, as are benefits, so employees may miss improvements, such as pay raises, they might have gotten automatically had they chosen to remain union-free.

I mention this because, at present, there are no time limits placed on negotiations, which means it could take months or even years for the union and the company to reach an agreement—and there are no guarantees that a contract will ever even be achieved. One study by MIT from a random selection of one thousand first-contract negotiations from all industries showed the following:

1. 25 percent of the time was the contract negotiated in the first year.
2. 75 percent of the time did the parties ever even reach a final contract.
3. 25 percent of the time, the parties never reached an agreement.
4. And finally, strikes occurred in 9 percent of first contract negotiations.

These are not facts and figures that employees are typically aware of when they are convinced that a union will immediately bring about the changes and promises the organizers have made. Collective bargaining is a concept that most employees have never heard of, much less understand how it works or the risks associated with it. And what happens if the union and management just cannot agree on a contract? Sometimes it's obvious to everyone that neither side is going to budge. At that point, the negotiations are at what's called an "Impasse."

An impasse gives the company the right to go ahead and start working under the terms of its final offer without the union's approval. This leaves the union with three choices: to give up; to give in, or to go on strike. Regardless of the outcome of collective bargaining, joining a union always has consequences, consequences that union organizers don't always make clear to employees beforehand.

Creating a union-proof environment means building an educated workforce—one that understands the risks involved in collective bargaining. A union-proof workforce won't fall for a union organizer's "promises" and is far more likely to work with management to solve their problems without the complications of a third party union getting involved.

Managing in a Union Environment

I want you to take on the role of a supervisor or manager for a moment… Let's say that you are making the rounds of your work area, and you encounter an employee named Alex just standing at his station without any work to do. After asking him how his kid's soccer team fared over the weekend, you then ask him to help another associate finish a rush order that has to go out today…

Alex replies: "I can't do that. Per our union contract, I'm not allowed to take on a different job position, even for a few hours, unless you have been given clearance first from the union—it's not currently part of my job description."

Unionization—it happens. And here's why you—and your front-line supervisors—have a direct personal stake in becoming a union-proof company.

The situation I just described with Alex may seem a bit extreme…but it does happen, and trying to manage in a unionized workplace can be both complex and challenging. In the case of Alex, flexibility, or the lack thereof, is a good example of some of those challenges. Such inflexibility quickly spreads over to affect cross-training.

Communication with employees is—at best—indirect, as it usually must involve a union representative. All of this translates to even more of the manager's time and effort to make it all work. The challenges of a unionized environment are frustrating, but they underscore the importance of maintaining a strong, trusting relationship with your union.

Yes, I said a "strong, trusting relationship with your union." For the sake of this discussion, let's assume that if a union exists in your company, you have both union and non-union employees. One important distinction to note is that the employees in the union are now "union members" and not "union employees." They are still *your* employees—not employees of the union.

Your leaders' excellent management skills and techniques will still apply to all employees. The company's guiding principles and mission statement do not change. Your managers must ask themselves how the presence of a union will affect his or her relationships with the employees. To ensure the integrity of your operation, it's better to position the union as a counterpart to your leadership team. Supervisors will communicate with your employees, and unions will communicate with their members.

So, consistent messaging is the greatest challenge to overcome. The problem is that union employees are, on average, less engaged in the company than non-union employees. According to a poll by Gallup's chief scientist for Workplace Management and Wellbeing, James K. Harter, Ph.D., the percentage of "actively disengaged" employees is considerably higher among unionized employees than among non-unionized employees within the same company. "Actively disengaged" workers aren't just unhappy; they're busy acting out that displeasure. Every day, actively disengaged workers undermine what their engaged, union-free coworkers accomplish.

The same data showed that unionized employees are more likely to say they will stay with their companies throughout their careers, but they're actually slightly less likely than their union-free counterparts to tell family and friends that it's a good place to work. In other words, the sense of security their union affiliation gives them may encourage unionized employees to stick around—

but that feeling doesn't translate into greater employee engagement with the company.

How can you build stronger engagement with your unionized employees? First, make your engagement-building process open, inclusive, and non-threatening. For example, if the company decides to undertake an employee engagement survey and a subsequent impact planning process, and unionized employees perceive this as secretive and threatening rather than constructive, the effort is essentially doomed from the start. Instead, it's vital to enlist the union's active support in such a survey and the resulting change processes.

Develop new lines of communication by using action planning with unionized employees. One reason union-management relations can be strained is that it's often hard to get everyone to agree on what's best for the workers. Using your engagement efforts as opportunities to find new ways to let employees speak for themselves is a great way to show that you're listening and that the outcome is important to you.

Many times the elephant in the room in making engagement work is the collective bargaining agreement. Remember, the collective bargaining agreement, or CBA is not a one-sided document. The CBA is a written and legally enforceable contract, set for a specified period—typically three years, but sometimes five—between management and its employees who are represented by the union. It sets down and defines the conditions of employment (including wages, working hours and conditions, overtime, holidays, vacation, benefits, and more), as well as procedures for dispute resolution. It may also be referred to as the labor agreement, union agreement, or union contract.

The CBA may be hundreds of pages long, and as I mentioned, it typically includes a Management Rights Clause. This clause sets out the rights reserved to the employer unless they are limited by other terms of the CBA. What does this mean? The Management Rights Clause gives company management the ability to manage its own business without interference from the union.

Remember, the employees are still *your* employees, and that means the company still has the right to hire employees, set work standards, control the work that is produced, and otherwise decide how the company will continue to remain profitable. Of course, a lot of the day-to-day management of employees falls squarely on the supervisors. To put this simply, your front-line leaders' primary function is ensuring that their employees are performing their jobs and performing them well. They must manage the performance…or poor performance will become the acceptable standard, the manager's reputation will be negatively impacted, and ultimately the business—and everyone who depends on its success—may suffer.

In a unionized environment, there are additional risks to address, including grievance processes and arbitrations. Both are time-consuming and costly. By addressing performance issues consistently, timely, and fairly, your management team will decrease the chances of encountering these more complex problems.

A grievance is any contract-related dispute or difference arising between the union and company management. It is usually filed on behalf of an employee (or employees) by the union. Grievance procedures vary, but the basic process involves a back-and-forth between the employee, the supervisor, and the shop steward or union representative, escalating to upper management on both sides. And if a solution still cannot be worked out at that point, a grievance goes to arbitration. Let's briefly review some of the key players and terms used in grievance procedures and arbitration.

Shop stewards, or union stewards, are employees of the company. They represent and defend the interests of their fellow employees, and they are elected by their union membership. Their duties typically include anything related to monitoring and enforcing the CBA, including all legal and regulatory requirements. They are the communication channels between the union and the employees. These stewards are employees who are paid by the company to participate in investigations, grievance hearings, disciplinary meetings, formal hearings, and employee negotiations.

Union representatives, on the other hand, are not employed by the company. Unions use these "organizers," or "business agents," to manage grievances and any related discussions along with the union stewards. In a union environment, any formal meeting between an employee and shop steward really must have a fellow manager or member of the human resources team present. And before a supervisor conducts any fact-finding interviews or imposes any disciplinary action, it's important to understand a unionized employee's rights under the law. Specifically, your management team needs to be familiar with what are called "Weingarten Rights."

Weingarten Rights were established in a 1975 NLRB case and briefly stated, say that employees who are covered by a CBA have the right to have a union representative or steward present at *any* meeting that might result in disciplinary action, including any fact-finding interviews. When arranging these types of meetings in a unionized environment, it is important to make sure that the employee is aware of what will be discussed in the meeting. Never retaliate against an employee for exercising their Weingarten Rights.

Another important thing to remember is that a good working relationship with the union steward is invaluable. Supervisors who gain the trust and respect of the union steward will find that the steward is more likely to come to them before any potential problems escalate into grievances. If you can do so, schedule regular and consistent meetings with your steward. Regular communication is essential in heading off issues, concerns, or other questions in the work unit.

I mentioned the word *trust* with regard to the shop steward, but this extends to all of the employees in the company. According to a survey by the American Psychological Association, one in four employees do not trust their employers. So, combine an existing trust problem with employees turning to a union, and you can see how a union might gain an advantage when it comes to your employee's interpretation of "open and honest" communication.

To build trust in a unionized environment, you may need to reevaluate your communication strategies. Nothing is stronger than effective communication, coupled with transparency, to foster trust and understanding with your employees. Arm your frontline management team so that they can serve as reliable sources of information and positive models of the company's culture for your unionized employees.

There is an adage that states: "Manage by walking around." It can be traced back to the management practices put into place at Hewlett-Packard in the 1970s, as well as outlined in the book "*In Search of Excellence: Lessons from America's Best-Run Companies* by Tom Peters and Robert H. Waterman." This refers to the practice of managers randomly wandering throughout the workplace in an unobstructed manner, to check in with employees, equipment, and processes regarding the status of ongoing work. The benefit of such a practice is that a manager is more likely to facilitate improvements to morale by a random sampling of events or employee discussions. Observing and interacting in this way also encourages greater productivity, a sense of organizational purpose, and total quality management of the organization. Bottom line: The more "face time" your leaders have with employees, the more likely they will be to turn to company representatives rather than a union representative to solve problems.

When company leaders take the time to meet with and talk to their employees, it creates a feeling that the management team genuinely cares about its employees. No one wants to hear or use the phrase, "the advantages of a unionized workplace," but, there are a few observations one can make from the perspective of unionized employees.

A union contract can provide a more predictable workplace for employees. Pursuing other opportunities is less important to unionized workers, especially if that opportunity will take them to a non-unionized environment. The resulting perception of stability means that there can be a reduction in the associated costs for hiring and onboarding new employees.

Many unionized workers become entitled to extended health and medical benefits through their union, and in today's healthcare marketplace, this can actually be an asset for both the employee and the company.

Additionally, according to the AFL-CIO, unions create higher productivity among a company's employees. Why? Thanks in part to reduced turnover, companies are more willing to bear the costs of providing extensive formalized job training, making workers more proficient at their jobs. Many times, workplace safety is also a component of contract negotiations. The assumption is that a safer environment means fewer injuries or accidents, so unionized companies may ultimately pay less in worker's compensation claims. These companies may also experience a reduction in absenteeism due to work-related injuries.

You may hear a lot about how union contracts try to stipulate procedures for disciplining employees—through alternative dispute resolution or grievance procedures. While this may ensure that employees are disciplined fairly and consistently, it also makes it difficult for employers to terminate those whom they may consider to be "problem" employees. However, the opposite side of this factor is that a dispute resolution process can protect companies from legal action taken by former employees who believe their firing was unjustified.

And finally, seniority can be an additional positive factor in determining who gets a promotion or even who gets to keep their jobs in the event of a period of layoffs. Although unions tell members that seniority can eliminate favoritism in the workplace, they often fail to mention the Super Seniority Clause frequently negotiated into most CBAs. Super Seniority rewards the union's shop steward by giving him or her the most seniority in the department, meaning that in the event of a layoff, they will be the last one to go.

These observations: a predictable workplace, better healthcare benefits, higher productivity, a safer work environment, a set structure for discipline, and seniority privileges are the *perceived* advantages of a unionized environment for many employees.

However, from a company perspective, unionization brings:
- Reduced flexibility
- Seniority controls
- Formal grievance process
- Union negotiations
- Possible strikes
- Increased legal costs

Some union members have learned how to abuse the system, discovering the loopholes or understanding that, thanks to the union grievance procedures, being fired from their position is highly unlikely. Morale can take a serious hit, therefore, as the CBA may reward employees regardless of their effort or work ethic. Many employees will immediately realize that pay-grade steps or planned raises are doled out equally to everyone, including union members who engage in work avoidance.

A similar feeling of *"I'm being held back"* can resonate with many employees regarding seniority in the workplace because the best person for the job ora promotion will be passed over because they don't have the seniority over a lesser-qualified associate who has simply been with the company for a longer period.

And finally, lingering tension between union and non-union employees left over from the campaign, or the now-constant battle to contain the union in a partially unionized workforce, can be very hard to shake.

These drawbacks reinforce the idea that knowledge is power—and nowhere is that more true than in a unionized workplace! To that end, know the law, and know your CBA better than the union does. The laws and rules that govern a unionized work environment are complex and vary widely. Become familiar with the laws and regulations that directly affect your organization and your team, and understand that assistance may be needed from labor counsel.

In addition, the supervisors in your newly unionized environment will need to learn to work with the shop stewards—the first level of representation for your union employees. The best practice is to work with them as though they are an extra set of eyes and ears for your leaders...much like a partner who is helping to manage your employees.

Finally, try to remember that for whatever reason, the union fulfills an important role for your employees. Respect that. Help them by keeping their good intentions at the forefront of any conversation or negotiation. This respect is good for the company, for the employees, for the union, and most importantly for you and your supervisors.

Consider another response that Alex could have made when asked by a supervisor to perform work outside of his "job description": "Sure thing, Rick. We'll have that order ready for pickup by five... You know, I'm available most afternoons, when they seem to have the greatest crunch times. Are there any opportunities for cross-training in that area? Which conversation would you prefer that your supervisor have with Alex? Create a union-proof environment in which employees have no reason to involve a third party in such conversations.

What Really Happens during a Strike?

A union strike is often referred to as the only real weapon a union has—but it is a weapon that can be devastating for everyone involved, and that alone should be reason enough to attempt to remain union-free.

For many of us, strikes aren't something about which we know a whole lot. Sure, we know that sometimes workers go on strike to force a company to agree to their demands—but how many of us have ever actually worked in a company where employees walked a picket line? It's something about which our parents and grandparents may have had to worry...but not us, not today—right?

Wrong.

While it's true that the frequency of strikes has declined over the years, it's important to remember that strikes *do* actually happen. In fact, nearly two thousand worker strikes occurred just between the years 2005 and 2014, involving more than 1.3 million workers, and strikes occur regardless of the union or industry in which your company is involved.

This means that even in today's economy, no unionized company, and no union-represented worker, can consider themselves safe from the threat of a union strike. Let's take a look at how strikes usually begin. Contrary to what unions may tell your employees, union strikes are generally not about the employees at all. They're about power.

Going back to collective bargaining, when a company and a union can't seem to reach an agreement on a contract, the two parties are at an impasse. An impasse leaves the union in a difficult position, and usually, they'll respond in one of three ways:

First, and by far the simplest way, is for the union to accept the contract, even if it might not include things they'd initially promised to their members.

Second, the union can simply give up. They could just walk away from the table and never come back—but often, this leaves employees worse off than before they were approached by the union.

Third and finally, in a desperate attempt to force the company into agreeing to their demands, the union can call a strike. Of course, the call to strike is usually not that simple. Often, the union first goes back to the employees and presents the company's "last, best contract" offer to them as a group, and the decision to strike is then put up for a vote. But even this relatively simple process contains some elements of concern.

Union organizers often lead employees to believe that they won't have to strike if they don't want to. But that's not entirely accurate. What *is* true is that some union members might get to decide by participating in a strike vote. Some, *but not all.* For instance, if a member isn't in good standing with the union, they might not be allowed to vote. And most union constitutions usually allow a strike to be called by the majority of the members "present and voting"—which sounds fair until you realize that this rule effectively allows a tiny percentage of the employee population to decide for the majority of the group.

For example, say a strike vote is held, but only ten people show up for the vote. Under the "present and voting" rule, just six people will make the decision on whether or not to strike—for everyone. If an employee can't make it to the particular meeting when the vote is held, well, that's just too bad. They'll find themselves out there on the picket line, just like everyone else.

If your company was unionized, you might even find your employees being strong-armed into participating in "sympathy strikes"—walking the picket line because employees in another company can't solve their problems.

And, finally, if the union believes your company has violated the CBA, they *can* call a strike against the employer—even without a vote! And your employees might have no choice but to walk out or face discipline from the union.

When a company's workers go on strike, three groups are immediately affected: the employees (and their families), the company, and the local community. Let's take a look at the impact a strike has on each of these groups individually. We'll start with the hardest-hit group, the employees themselves.

During an economic strike, employees on the picket line are the first to feel the financial impact of the action—in the following ways:

- Paychecks from the company immediately stop coming into the employees on strike.
- Employees on strike may have to pay the entire premium for any medical insurance policies.
- Economic strikers don't qualify for unemployment in many states.

The union might have some strike funds set aside for picketing workers—but in recent years, many unions have diverted these funds to organizing efforts or to union elections. Even if they do have funds for strikers available, it's often far less than strikers might anticipate. Union members are generally shocked to learn that a strike fund might only pay $50 to $75 a week per striker—and what's more, throughout the strike, picketing workers are often still expected to pay their union dues!

Employees whose unions call them out on strike may have something else to worry about: their job security. While the union has the right to strike, your company also has the right to keep on operating, which means that you, as the company, have the right to hire replacement workers to do the strikers' jobs.

The NLRB has stated that "an employer may permanently replace economic strikers." Therefore, once the strike ends—*if* it ends—those replacement workers can actually keep the strikers' jobs for as long as they want them. Finally, you'll notice that I just said "*if* the strike ends"—because when a union goes on strike, there's no real way to predict how long it might last... Strikes are not held to any time limit except for what the strikers are willing to endure. That means that your company might have to face a strike that lasts for days, months, or even years...

We've seen how strikes pose potential risks to both the strikers' financial and job security, but they also constitute a risk to your employees' personal safety, to their health and security. On a picket line, striker frustration can quickly build into anger, and all too often this ends in violence. During strikes, employees can and do get hurt. Just ask former University of Miami football star Rod Carter. He was a Teamster union member, and when his union went on strike against his company, UPS, he crossed the picket line and suffered five stab wounds as a result.

Clearly, your employees have a lot to lose in the event of a union strike. But what about your company—the intended target of the union's action? That answer depends on how proactive your company has been in prepping for the possibility of a strike. Companies can certainly be hurt by a strike, in many of the same ways that employees can. With workers on a picket line, your production or delivery of services can be delayed, leaving customers in the lurch. As a result, your customers may opt to find other vendors, and they may not make the effort to come back when the strike is over. The financial impact of that client migration can be significant, and it often forces companies to introduce cost-cutting measures, to initiate layoffs, and even to move work to other facilities. , Your managers may be required to fill in on the floor to keep up with client demand, working side by side with any replacement workers. And as "collateral damage" in a strike, your managers may experience the same risks that striking employees do—the risks of violence and damaged working relationships.

Last, but certainly not least, entire communities are impacted by the economic and social effects of a union strike—and the smaller the community, generally the harder the impact a strike will have. Let's take a look at how this can occur.

Money lost by employees and companies is also money lost to the community. Schools, parks, and even future generations can suffer as a result of this loss of revenue. Communities can be further impacted if the striking company is one that provides critical services to residents. Strikes that affect hospitals or schools, for example, can bring communities to a standstill, kicking off a domino effect of disruption. And, of course, the community can become socially divided by a strike, as people start taking sides and holding grudges that can change the very nature of the community as a whole.

You should already understand the economic impact a strike can have on a company and its workforce. Sometimes that impact can be hard to assess without actual numbers attached to it. In 2008, 27,000 union-represented machinists went out on strike against aircraft maker Boeing, over wages, benefits, and outsourcing of jobs. The strike lasted eight weeks, costing each striking employee an average of seven thousand dollars in lost base pay. Multiply that out, and you will find that a total of $189,000,000 were lost by those 27,000 striking workers.

Also, the strike cost the company $100,000,000 *per day* in lost revenue and in the penalties they incurred for not meeting their clients' delivery deadlines.

Now, that was just the cost of an *eight-week* strike—so just imagine what their costs might have been if their strike had followed the same timeline as the strike at Chicago's Congress Plaza Hotel.

In 2003, 130 cleaning and maintenance workers at the historic hotel went on strike, protesting a proposed wage cut. Workers took to the picket lines…but *ten years later*, there was *still* no agreement. When the union finally called an end to the strike, the company was as surprised as anyone, because they had not sat down at the negotiation table with the union in over a year.

What was the result of this ten-year strike? When the strike ended, the citywide standard pay for the room attendants was $16.40 an hour. The union told the few dozen workers who were still on strike that they could be fully reinstated at their jobs—at the same pay rate they had when they went on strike in 2003: *$8.83 an hour.*

Unionized companies face the possibility of this nightmare scenario every time they enter contract negotiations, typically every three years. But there are some things your company can do in advance to ensure that, should a strike occur, you're as well-prepared as you can be.

The key to managing a strike is advanced planning. Most strikes take place when labor contracts expire, so there are usually no big surprises about the timing of a possible strike. Strike preparation plans must cover a wide spectrum of business areas, including:
- Contingency workforce planning
- Appropriate training programs in place for contingency workers
- Interim policies covering human resources issues, for both striking and non-striking workers
- Customer and supplier communication plans in the event of a strike announcement

- Planned provision of alternative services for valued clients in the event of a strike
- A security plan that provides managers and non-striking employees safe passage to and from the workplace, while at the same time allowing for the gathering of evidence of any strike-related misconduct for use in potential legal proceedings

Your company, your employees, and the communities in which you live and operate can suffer shocking losses in the wake of a labor action. While advance planning can help unionized companies manage the unpredictable and expensive consequences of a strike, even with a plan in place, one thing is still clear: The only sure way to avoid a union strike is to avoid a union altogether. And that's ultimately why your company is making the effort to become a union-proof company.

Chapter 6

Getting Union-Proof

Resources

Becoming union-proof is more than just understanding unions and how they work. It's also about anticipating union actions and preparing your company against future organizing attempts by unions.

Knowing what resources are available is one component while understanding how they work together can be the key to winning. The path to becoming union-proof begins with understanding that this is not something your company needs to do all on its own. There are many outstanding collaborative resources available to help—people who understand the nature of labor relations and who specialize in ways to protect, defend, and assist companies and their employees in staying union-free.

We'll begin with lawyers. A labor law attorney represents employers or individuals involved in legal disputes, generally over the terms and conditions of employment. Your labor attorney might be in private practice; they might work for a law firm, or they might be employed directly by your company as in-house counsel.

Labor law in the United States is anything but straightforward. It can become complicated and it is constantly changing. It can help to have a legal team on hand if you become involved in union organizing, contract negotiations, or any defense of labor conflicts. There is no way for an individual or even a company to be fully prepared to confront a union without specialized legal expertise—and that includes going before the NLRB, federal or national mediation boards, your state labor board, or the court system.

The value of a good labor attorney becomes even more evident the moment a union-organizing campaign begins. Regardless of size, any company that hears early whispers of a union campaign should engage counsel immediately. Employment attorneys will help you understand the law and keep all of your actions legal. Also, some firms even specialize in union avoidance, and they can help guide you to improve your chances of remaining union-free if you're ever challenged with an organizing campaign. Some companies even have full-time, in-house labor attorneys, whose sole purpose is to help keep a company union-free. Their full-time attention to ever-changing labor laws, the particular dynamics your company, its issues, and its employees can be vital to the effectiveness of your union-proofing efforts.

Labor attorneys are essential, either in-house or on-call, but attorneys aren't the only professionals you will want to employ in your effort to push back against a union. Labor consultants have proven themselves to be critical to the success of many labor campaigns, crafting custom campaign strategies for businesses that are designed to educate employees as well as win over their hearts and minds. Professional labor consultants work with companies to address and fight union-organizing efforts. While they don't offer legal advice, they can advise you on your strategies and present options for "next steps" if an organizing campaign progresses.

Consultants traditionally remain in the background of a campaign, working with your labor attorneys and other employee communication experts to help you educate your employees without incurring ULP charges. Consultants work with supervisors and management personnel, coaching them on talking points, brainstorming company communications, and otherwise helping to move things toward a successful resolution. Like attorneys, labor consultants can prove to be valuable allies in your effort to create a union-proof culture. Labor consultants can assist your company with strategies to remain competitive, by helping you minimize labor costs and maximize productivity. These specialists may participate in contract negotiations, help respond to corporate campaigns, and even help craft strike contingency plans, if necessary.

Sometimes companies will ask, "What is the difference between hiring a labor attorney and hiring a labor consultant?" Or, "Should I ever hire both at the same time?" The lines of responsibility here can become blurred. After all, a lawyer can consult, but a consultant would have to go to law school to become a lawyer!

All kidding aside, labor lawyers can provide a better perspective on legal matters, typically based on law or precedent case law. This point of view then guides their clients' decision-making process. Labor consultants do not need to base their advice on the law. Legal regulations can be a subset of a consultant's advice, and in fact, many times they will consult the attorney on the team. Typically, the advice an expert dispenses is based on their experience, best practices, and lots of data analysis. At times, basic common sense is a consultant's best strategy, simply because they have a wealth of experience having dealt with similar situations. For example, some consultants are actually ex-union organizers or former union members, and that "insider knowledge" can provide them with a unique perspective.

Both labor consultants and attorneys can make an impact on your company's union-proofing efforts, but there's a third resource that brings their efforts together and can make your company's messages resonate with your employees, and that is employee communication experts.

Employee communication experts are professional communicators who also may specialize in labor relations and connecting with employees. They are writers and artists, media producers and web architects, and a whole host of other specialists who stand ready to help you find the right words and the right media messages to use. Employee communication experts may produce videos, build websites, write speeches, design handouts, maintain blogs, and coordinate social media efforts, all targeted at helping to keep your company union-free. These different professionals are accustomed to both the timeline and the tone of labor messaging so that your communication stays on time and on topic. And if a union presents an organizing campaign or even a corporate campaign, your employee communication expert will be ready to respond, working with your team and the attorneys and consultants you choose to meet your changing communication needs.

Many employee communication experts offer specialized resources that will help you to keep your workforce engaged and motivated, crafting training materials, onboarding strategies, and even labor relations education for supervisors and employees. The best employee communication experts have vast labor relations experience to assist in every type of labor situation. They know that both messaging and timing matter, they can provide a wide variety of options to deliver your message, and they can even help you to reach home audiences, using social media and other powerful online tools. Similar to the attorneys or consultants that you hire, your employee communication experts will enable you and your team to focus on your union-proof strategies and help you to maintain a direct connection with your employees.

However, you need to be aware that anytime any of your resource providers undertake activities with the intent to "directly" persuade your employees concerning their right to organize and bargain collectively, they become classified by the U.S. Department of Labor as "persuaders." Persuaders - and employers who hire them - must file specific DOL reports. I recommend visiting the U.S. Department Of Labor's website for the latest information on these reports, forms and instructions for filing.

I think it is important to know that the DOL attempted to alter the Persuader Rule in 2016. The DOL wanted employers that utilize any assistance with the intent to "directly *or indirectly*" persuade employees to report this information to the DOL. The words to pay particular attention to are "directly" and "indirectly." "Directly" classifies a particular kind of provider, while "indirectly" basically means every resource provider. Now, the DOL attempted to alter the Persuader Rule, but a U.S. District Court in Texas provided an order granting injunctive relief nationwide on June 27, 2016. Of course, the problem with an injunctive relief is that someday the Persuader Rule may come back in one form or another to the satisfaction of the court. With that said, the following section is written as if the Persuader Rule were allowed to move forward, as I want you to have this valuable information, should it come back to life.

The 2016 Persuader Rule changed the requirements for employers and their resources regarding the filing of official reports with the DOL. You need to understand these rules when you hire any provider to help your company stay union-free.

The law now requires employers like you to file a report with the Department of Labor whenever you hire anyone with the intent of connecting with employees on the issue of unionization. Here's a bit of history about this subject: From 1962 through 2015, the Department of Labor recognized an "advice exception" to the reporting requirement, which provided that no report would be necessary if a resource provider were simply providing "advice" to the employer or company. For years, the DOL interpreted the "advice exception" broadly, excluding the need to report, as long as the outside resources a company hired had no *direct contact* with its employees.

However, in 2016, the DOL significantly narrowed its interpretation of that "advice exception." Under the newly revised rules, this exception now applies only to a very particular collection of legal advice. What that means for you as an employer is that you need to be aware of all reporting requirements before engaging any outside resources on the topic of unionization. Many companies are unaware of the Persuader Rule and the filing requirements until it is time to engage these outside resources. Knowing what's required ahead of time allows you to take full advantage of the knowledge available—without any fear of the reporting requirements.

Why would companies fear this reporting? To begin with, the reports force a union-proof company and its resources to make confidential information public, information that might later be used by a union against that employer. This means that some companies that feel their brands might be harmed by association with any union-avoidance activities may cease those activities altogether, or bring them in-house, so as to avoid the reporting requirements. Other companies may feel that this rule violates their attorney-client relationship, resulting in their hesitation to even consult with legal counsel, even when they really need it, thus opening themselves up to costly lawsuits for unintentional violations of labor laws and regulations.

The U.S. Department of Labor will tell you that the rule "provides employees with information about the use of labor relations consultants by employers, both openly and behind the scenes, to shape how employees exercise their union representation and collective bargaining rights." However, the real reason is to create a chilling effect on employers' free speech and lead to a reduction in the willingness of employers to seek resource assistance when they and their employees need it most.

However, the value that qualified professional resources, such as attorneys, consultants, and employee communication experts, can bring to a company far outweighs any downside of the DOL's reporting requirements. The fact is, labor campaigns are rarely won alone. Attorneys will keep you within the letter of the law. Consultants will design a winning game plan, and employee communication experts will make sure that your message is well-received by your audience. The more expert help you have, the more diverse your ideas will be and the more strategies from which you'll be able to choose. The collective experience of your resources can guide you to solutions and responses that you might not have considered on your own, and in the end, these might just be the very thing that tips the election in your favor and keeps your company union-free.

The final resource category you'll find incredibly helpful is trade associations. Interestingly enough, trade associations get a break in what must be reported to the Department of Labor. Membership in an association is not considered "persuader activity." Newsletters from a trade association - even with labor information sent to all members - will not trigger any reporting obligations. Trade associations may also provide you with advice on "off-the-shelf" materials regarding union avoidance without reporting. Some examples of industry-specific trade associations include:
- Retail Industry Leaders Association
- National Association of Manufacturers
- North American Transportation Employee Relations Association
- Associated Builders and Contractors
- International Franchise Association

Some trade associations are not industry-specific, but they offer similar benefits. Organizations such as this include:
- U.S. Chamber of Commerce
- Society for Human Resource Management
- CUE

Becoming a member of any of these organizations will allow you to access valuable information, will keep you informed on any changing legislation and rules, and perhaps even more important, will provide access to other like-minded individuals willing to share best practices in human resources and labor relations.

Researching the best resources for your company in advance of any labor situation is almost always the best strategy for your union-proof company...far preferable to trying to build a labor team on the fly in a reactive situation.

To get started, you'll want to immediately locate the best labor attorney or law firm in your area. For this process, you need to understand the difference between an attorney and a consultant, as well as when each of these strategists might be useful to you, either alone or together. You'll also want to find employee communication experts with extensive human resources and labor relations experience. These resources are critical to engaging employees in your union-proofing efforts. Remember that the best strategy and the best message in the world are worthless if you can't connect with your employees.

Finally, connect with like-minded companies who are willing to learn and share their knowledge through trade, industry, or interest-based associations. Next, I will share a process that helps companies access and analyze employee attitudes to build a better understanding of a companies' union risk via a Vulnerability Assessment.

Vulnerability Assessments

The engagement between companies and employees is critical to the success of any business, and that connection is vital to creating a union-proof culture. Maintaining your relationship with your employees requires effort. You need to routinely observe your workplace with a careful eye, not just for signs of an organizing campaign, but also for any changes that might make your employees more vulnerable to the advances of a union.

Every employee comes to work with his or her attitude toward the company and their job. Employees may be engaged in the work they do, they may "buy in" to the direction of the company, they might be totally aligned with the corporate culture—or they might not. Understanding these employee attitudes is useful for any company, for any number of reasons, but it is particularly helpful in trying to gauge a group's possible receptiveness to union messaging. Vulnerability assessment is the process that helps companies access and analyze employees' attitudes to build a better understanding of the company's overall susceptibility.

Now, this process may seem like something only large companies would need to invest in, but really, this process can be beneficial to any organization. Who, then, should engage in vulnerability assessments?

- Any union-free company that wishes to avoid unionization.
- Any unionized company seeking to determine workforce readiness for decertification.
- Any company, non-union or union, looking for more ways to be proactive and responsive to employees' needs.
- Any company that suspects they may be vulnerable for any reason, or in need of some threat or risk analysis.

Vulnerability assessments serve as a kind of "early warning system," alerting you as to when the conditions might be ripe for an organizing drive. These alerts can help you identify and address areas of concern—before a union ever gets involved. This can potentially prevent an organizing campaign from taking root. A well-executed assessment can provide you with a sense of how likely union activity is to occur, and if it did occur, how likely it would be to succeed.

Although the value of an assessment is clear, many companies simply don't engage in this process. Why? The range of objections include:

- They don't know what's involved in the process.
- They don't want to invest the time needed to conduct a proper in-house assessment.
- They feel they already have a solid grasp on the mood of their employees.
- They're hesitant to make the investment with a professional assessment team.

This is a false economy, of both time and money, because by refusing to invest in some form of vulnerability assessment, you unwittingly open the door to a host of even more damaging possibilities. When a company refuses to engage in a vulnerability assessment, they miss the opportunity to address issues before a union comes to call. It not only leaves the door open for union activity, but it also prevents companies from understanding how vulnerable they are to union organizing in the first place, leaving them unprepared to defend themselves when a union campaign begins.

The important thing to remember is to weigh the cost of an assessment against the cost of unionization. Your investment in a vulnerability assessment is far more economical than a later expense of dealing with a reactive situation, or worse, becoming a unionized operation.

Convincing the corporate suite of this investment may be your first challenge, but in the meantime, let's take a closer look at how these assessments are conducted, and by whom. Ideally, a vulnerability assessment should be a team effort, involving members of your company's Human Resources department, your Employee or Labor Relations department, and your Operations department, all working in conjunction with outside professional assessment resources.

Professional vulnerability assessment providers are not only well-versed in the assessment process, but they have the advantage of being able to see your organization from the outside, free from any expectations or bias. By collaborating with your internal teams, assessment providers can create a comprehensive model of your company's vulnerability to labor unions. Of course, you can conduct a vulnerability assessment internally, and many providers offer management training so that you can conduct an evaluation on your own.

Vulnerability assessment is an observation-based process that strives to build an accurate, fact-based view of a company's current susceptibility to labor unions. And while it may be tempting to think that susceptibility begins and ends with employees, that would be leaving out some other critical factors.

For a precise evaluation, vulnerability assessment must take into consideration not only what goes on inside a company, but also what happens on the outside. In fact, an external review is sometimes the recommended starting point for your assessment. External assessments are centered around three critical factors: your company's location, its industry, and its market.

Your location assessment begins by observing the businesses and the personnel working in your company's vicinity that may be influencing your employees. If any neighboring businesses have recently lost a union campaign, or if a local unionized company has recently made some large concessions during contract negotiations, pro-union sentiment may still be in the air locally, prompting your employees to think more positively of unions. On the other hand, if unionized workers in the area have had any negative experiences—including strikes, layoffs, or closings that weren't mitigated by their union presence—that can have a lasting impact on your workforce, as well.

The same goes for industry trends. Unions often target companies based on industry alone, so your assessment should address whether or not these trends might impact the way your employees perceive unions. Employees working in heavily unionized trades may not feel "professional" without a union card in their wallets, whereas employees working in less labor-represented areas may find the idea of a union too "blue collar." These preconceptions can have an unyielding impact on your company's vulnerability to unionization.

Finally, your market should be considered. How is your company viewed as an employer in the local community? Generally speaking, companies that are deemed to be "employers of choice"—offering competitive wages and benefits, good working environments, and job stability—are less vulnerable to labor unions than those with less-than-stellar reputations in the local community. Being an employer of choice and being union-proof typically go hand in hand!

Your external assessment sets the stage, much of its consideration relating to realities that are outside of your company's control. These factors can affect your union-proofing efforts, and understanding them will give you greater visibility to the challenges your organization may face.

Now, let's move on to the internal process. An internal assessment should begin with a review of your company's associations with labor unions. Any past or present union representation should be noted, as should any union campaigns, whether they were won or lost by the company. This review will give you an idea whether any loyalties (to unions) or prejudices (against unions) exist within your ranks. Knowing which exist—and to what extent—can be very helpful in the event of a union campaign. Your assessment should include a review of any unionized units within your company, to evaluate their potential readiness for decertification.

This should be followed by a review of your actual workplace. This can be accomplished through simple observation: Is the location well-maintained? Is it safe? Is the equipment that the employees use up-to-date and fully operational? If the answer to any of these questions is no, then morale may be suffering, and that can lead to your employees supporting union representation to motivate change from management.

For similar reasons, internal trends in other workplace issues, such as job turnover, on-the-job accidents, customer satisfaction, and even issues concerning ethics or trust, need to be reviewed, as well. Professional assessors may conduct interviews with the Operations and Human Resources departments to provide a comprehensive understanding of any areas of concern. Professional vulnerability consultants will make an effort to gain a general understanding of who your employees are, what their backgrounds are, and any other details and factors that might indicate their openness toward unionization. For example, people who have been passed over for promotions are more likely to see union representation as a good thing. Short-term employees tend to be more prone to voting in unions than long-term employees. The more information a vulnerability consultant can gather to help understand your specific workforce, the more accurate your assessment will be.

This is also an ideal time to check out your company's online reputation, especially as it relates to your particular location. You can set-up Google alerts rather easily, and your vulnerability consultants will likely do some specialized online research for any red flags. They may visit websites like Glassdoor.com and Indeed.com, which allow the public to post reviews of their employers, as well as other "Bash the Boss" sites like coworker.org, jobschmob.com, and reddit.com, for any further relevant content about your company.

Again, your internal assessment is all about gathering intelligence and building a deeper understanding of how your company is perceived by people both inside and outside of the organization. Once all of the background research has been compiled, then it is time for the fieldwork.

Assessors will be quick to tell you that the most valuable insights in this process tend to come as a result of the field assessments because the information received there comes straight from the mouths of your employees. Field assessment is done in two ways—through actual one-on-one discussions with employees and through anonymous employee surveys.

First, assessors will go into the workplace and simply speak with the employees—asking for their opinions about the company, about management, and about any other issues surrounding their jobs and their workplace. These conversations can be very enlightening, and when correctly conducted, they can open up some great communication with your workforce.

Anonymous employee surveys are a critical part of any successful field assessment, and they should cover the same topics as the one-on-one interviews. The hope is that the anonymous nature of the surveys will allow employees to open up even more, to be even more frank, and to share their real thoughts without fear of repercussion or judgment.

Please note that neither the in-person discussions nor the anonymous surveys should ask employees directly about unions. However, your management team may be called upon to share their impressions as to whether they think their team might be vulnerable to unionization.

It should also be noted that unless you conduct regular—say, annual—field assessments, you should not undertake one during an active union campaign, to avoid any potential ULPs or even just the appearance of impropriety. Regular field evaluations, both the discussions and the surveys, will do more than just contribute to understanding your employee vulnerability to unions, however. They will also help you to establish a routine of gaining feedback from employees. Supporting this kind of consistent involvement with your employees sends two very strong messages to the employees: first, that your company is willing to listen and that it cares about their concerns, and second, that the company stands ready to provide them with clear, confidential channels they can use to have their voices heard. This is particularly the case when you choose to have your assessments conducted by an *outside* professional assessment team, as that adds a layer of neutrality to the process.

At its core, vulnerability assessment is about more than just prepping for a potential union campaign; it's about establishing a conversation with your employees, and as part of your union-proofing efforts, it's about being proactive about their concerns. Professional companies, such as Spring International, suggest that companies conduct a vulnerability assessment at least once or twice a year to maintain the best understanding of their positions. When assessments are carried out on that schedule, they can become a kind of corporate "checkup," alerting management to any areas of concern and ways that morale might be better maintained.

Whether you choose to go it on your own, or you engage a professional team of assessors, conducting regular vulnerability assessments is a critical component in building your union-proof workplace culture.

Employee Handbooks and Policies

"Employees...have the right to form, join or assist a union." Have you ever read the National Labor Relations Act? Of course not—it's not one of those great, inspired business books. But understanding it may be the most vital part of your union-proofing efforts.

Why?

Well, consider this...

"Workers have the right to organize a union to negotiate with their employer over terms and conditions of employment. This includes the right to distribute union literature, wear union buttons, T-shirts, or other insignia (except in unusual "special circumstances"), solicit co-workers to sign union authorization cards, and discuss the union with coworkers."

It continues: "Supervisors and managers cannot spy on employees (or make it appear that they are doing so), coercively question them, threaten, or bribe them regarding union organizing activity or the union activities of co-workers. They cannot be fired, disciplined, demoted, or penalized in any way for engaging in these activities."

And here's where the rules get even more interesting. The NLRA states that working time is for work, so the company may maintain and enforce nondiscriminatory rules limiting solicitation and distribution. But you *can't* prohibit employees from discussing union representation when they're aren't working. That means that before or after work or during break times you cannot prevent them from soliciting or distributing pro-union literature. This applies to the location as well. You cannot stop them from solicitation and distribution in non-work areas, such as parking lots or break rooms.

Is your head spinning yet? Well, the NLRB has recently cracked down on employee handbooks and the policies they outline. You need to know what that means for your company.

Do you have a company handbook, with policies in place that prevent a union from using your employees to do their organizing business on company time? If you haven't reviewed those policies within the last year, the odds are good that your handbook and policies are actually ticking time bombs. The NLRB would very likely find your outdated policies in violation of your employees' Section 7 rights, and if they do so, it will certainly generate stress for you at the least, and more likely bring about ULPs for the company.

Let's review some definitions and general concepts concerning solicitation and distribution before we go a little deeper. *Solicitation* deals with speech, and it centers on conversations in which employees speak to each other about their favorite causes, whether it's "soliciting" fellow employees to come to a church bazaar—or to go to a union meeting. *Distribution* involves printed materials, such as charity event announcements—or union handouts. The rule as to when employees are permitted to solicit (talk about unions) or distribute (union materials) is essentially the same: Solicitation conversations and distribution of literature can take place only in non-work areas during non-working times.

So, that's the distinction between the two—solicitation and distribution—and the textbook definition for each, but what you need to understand is what solicitation and distribution policies look like in action, both for your employees and for non-employees, such as union organizers.

Your employees have the legal right to support a union and engage in related activities, those "Section 7" activities about which I've talked. But companies *are* allowed to limit those activities in certain circumstances. For example, if an employee is on their break, and they're talking about the union with another employee who's still doing company work, your managers are allowed to stop the solicitation of the still-working employee. Your supervisors and managers should know that if either solicitation or distribution occurs during work, then they should politely ask the employees to resume their jobs rather than engaging in those activities. In the case of distribution, your managers should never request or demand to take away any materials the employees may possess. They shouldn't ask any questions of employees related to the activity—be sure they observe the T.I.P.S. rule!

Plus, remember that "casual" conversations among employees regarding the union are *not* considered solicitation, and it cannot be prohibited at any time—including in work or sales areas. That means that if your manager overhears a general conversation taking place about the benefits or drawbacks of unionization, but there is no *actual* discussion explicitly encouraging card signing or attendance at a meeting, that is protected, concerted activity, and it is *not* covered by the solicitation and distribution policies.

Union organizers or outside supporters are allowed to solicit and distribute to employees—but they must do so off of company premises. If anyone at your company observes non-employees talking to employees or handing out union literature off of company premises, they *cannot* approach them or ask them to stop—*unless* they directly come onto company property.

If non-employee organizers *are* on company property, then your managers should immediately inform you so that you can take the appropriate steps to address this unauthorized conduct and ensure that non-employees leave the premises right away.

Here's how you'll need to maintain a written "solicitation and distribution" policy in your employee handbook or personnel manuals. Your policy needs to be carefully worded to restrict the times and places where employees might solicit or distribute non-work materials to other employees. It is vital that you consistently enforce your solicitation and distribution policies carefully, with no exceptions or favoritism (even with non-union issues), so as not to create an opening for a union to claim that they, too, have the right to solicit on company property. This includes limiting activities related to charitable causes in which your employees may be involved.

In the past, taking care around solicitation and distribution issues was more about the actions a company might take. But today, your actions are just half of the equation; the other half is how the policy is written in the first place. This is the latest target on which the NLRB has chosen to focus their attention on behalf of employees.

As an example, Mercedes-Benz thought their handbook policy on solicitation and distribution of materials was clear and easy to understand:

"It is the goal of Mercedes to produce the highest quality vehicle at the most competitive cost. Activities which interfere with these efforts cannot be permitted. Mercedes prohibits solicitation and/or distribution of non-work-related materials by Team Members during work time or in working areas."

Pretty straightforward, right? The NLRB disagreed, invalidating the policy. The Board decided that Mercedes' policy was overly broad, and therefore a potential threat to workers' Section 7 rights.

The Board, therefore, ordered Mercedes-Benz to:

"1. Rescind the rule in its employee handbook that prohibited solicitation of employees not on working time by other employees not on working time in working areas;
2. Furnish employees with an insert for the current employee handbook, or publish and distribute to employees a revised employee handbook, with a lawfully worded solicitation and distribution policy; and
3. Post notices of its violation in conspicuous areas of the workplace for sixty days."

Another danger of your solicitation and distribution policy can be thinking it could be used to stop organizing activity. As an example of this, Conagra Foods issued a verbal warning to one employee for what they believed was a violation of the company's non-solicitation policy. The employee in question had a brief verbal exchange on the production floor, in which she informed two coworkers that they could find the union authorization cards they had requested in a particular locker.

Because the "violation" occurred during work hours and in a work area, Conagra posted a letter stating that its solicitation policy also covered union "discussions" and that those discussions were limited to non-working times. The NLRB actually had no issue with Conagra's no-solicitation policy... Instead, the Board concluded that the employee's actions simply did not constitute "solicitation" under Board law.

According to the Board, a mere mention of union authorization cards during work time does*n't* qualify as solicitation. The Board stated that solicitation, "means asking someone to join the union by signing an authorization card." Asking for a signature prompts an immediate response and presents a greater potential for interference with the productivity of employees who are supposed to be working.

Because the employees' brief interaction contained no signature request and no cards were actually presented, there was no "request for action" and therefore no risk of interference with production. Therefore, absent solicitation, Conagra's verbal warning was deemed to be an interference with the employee's right under the NLRA to engage in protected union activity. Yes, it was a section 7 violation.

The Board then took it one step further by concluding that the letter posted by Conagra to all employees was unlawful because employees could view it as barring all "discussions" during work time. So again, the Board's position was that "most discussions about unions are just that—discussions, not solicitations—and therefore the letter's expansive limitation of union-related discussions to non-working time was thus overbroad and unlawful under the Act."

One more example - Target's no-solicitation/no-distribution policy prohibited employees at all times from "solicitation, and distribution of literature if they are for commercial profit." The NLRB found that prohibiting solicitation and distribution "at all times" for "commercial purpose" could be read as prohibiting solicitation and distribution regarding union membership. As I've mentioned, the NLRA allows employers to prohibit solicitation by employees during work time, but during non-work time, companies cannot stop employees from soliciting. Bottom line: Employers may not enforce a blanket rule barring any or all solicitation by employees.

To create your own company's policies, first, you'll want to review and correct any no-solicitation policy that does not clearly follow the limits established by the Board: non-work time, and non-work area. Develop, implement, and administer your policy in such a way that employees could never reasonably conclude that their right to engage in protected concerted activity is limited, whether it is union-related or not. Any ambiguities need to be eliminated, as vague or unclear language could be interpreted as being "overly broad." When possible violations of your policy arise, before administering any level of discipline, you'll need to evaluate the specifics. Without a direct request to sign a union authorization card or an actual presentation of a card, discussions that simply mention a union, or even include an invitation to a union meeting, would be unlikely to be considered "lawfully disciplinable conduct," as was mentioned in the case of Conagra.

Next, you'll want to evaluate any areas of your facilities that need to be defined as "work areas," "non-work areas," or "mixed-use areas." If a zone is a non-work or a mixed-use area, you cannot stop protected activity there, unless that activity interferes with production or work performance. Remember the Mercedes-Benz case? One of the other issues, in that case, was about the definition of whether the space in question (where the solicitation occurred) was classified as a mixed-use area or a work area. It turned out to be mixed-use and thus a violation.

Some of the time, union organizing is all about leaflets and meetings, both of which the solicitation and distribution rule profoundly impacts. But today, online union organizing is just as prevalent, with organizing via e-mail, through texting, and on social media. Greater numbers of employees are using social media, and that means they're naturally engaging in protected, concerted activities anytime they talk/write about work. Their complaints about managers or companies now reach millions of people, including your customers and clients. So, what can you do about this?

Social media policies or even actions taken toward employees regarding social media issues are the NLRB's newest area of attack. And, upon closer examination of many social media cases, they tend to play out in much the same way as the employee handbook and policies, e-mail, and solicitation and distribution violations, in that the findings by the Board typically confirm some type of interference with the employee's Section 7 rights.

Costco Wholesale Corporation encountered the United Food and Commercial Workers Union, which filed ULP charges for perceived violations of the NLRA. The union called into question an "electronic posting rule" in the Costco employee handbook, which advised employees that posting anything damaging to the company or any employee was a violation of company policy.

Do you see any problems with this policy? If you said no, then the ALJ when the case was first presented agreed with you... But the union appealed, and the NLRB decided that Costco's employee policies were "too broad" to cover use of the internet and social media. The panel ruled that these policies "effectively stifle its employees' right to free speech under the Act."

Then there's the case involving Landry's, Inc., which operates several companies, including Bubba Gump Shrimp Restaurants. Landry's social media policy included limitations on postings that might damage the morale of employees or the reputation of the company, stating that employees should be "civil" to one another online. Sounds reasonable, right?

The NLRB's General Counsel determined the policy prohibited protected activity for employees. Landry's appealed, and in the end, the NLRB concluded that the words "morale" and "being civil to others and their opinions" were meant to regulate the tone—not the content—of employee postings and that Bubba Gump's policy, therefore, did *not* violate the NRLA. What is the takeaway from all of this?

Review your social media policies as soon as possible with your legal counsel for any potential violations. Consider including language that specifically defines "protected concerted activities" under the NLRA. The NLRB's General Counsel issues a helpful document that outlines cases annually, which you may want to review. One from April 2015 published by NLRB General Counsel was, "Helpful Guidance on Employee Handbook Policies and Rules." That document showed that language regarding employee social media use is typically problematic, including policies that use words such as "prohibit," "require," "discourage," "encourage," or "threaten." What that means for you is that diligence and legal counsel is likely needed when defining your policies.

The employee handbook is where most of these rules, statements, and policies are outlined for employees to review from day one via your onboarding program. The number of topics in employee handbooks varies from company to company, and the NLRB is very interested in every single one of the subjects that you are covering with your employees. Similar to what I have already discussed, the issues the Board takes up with employee handbooks are not so much concerning the rules themselves, but first, how they are written, and second, how an employee could interpret what you are saying. Any language that violates or even "chills" an employee concerning their Section 7 rights is eventually going to be a problem.

Solicitation and distribution rules, rules concerning e-mail use, social media policies, and employee handbooks are probably the most fluid of any topic in this book. Make sure that you stay informed, alert, and aware as you make proactive and informed decisions in these areas.

Getting Proactive: Preventive Measures

A large part of becoming union-proof is making sure that you're the kind of company that doesn't need a union. If your employees understand that your company is already treating them well without union intervention, then you're ahead of the game.

When I mention being proactive, I mean that you should become the kind of company for which people *want* to work. A company that is not proactive is in the constant position of putting out fires and of reacting to external forces, rather than expending energy in the right direction—to grow the company and every employee who works for it.

As part of the team responsible for union-proofing your company, you need to start thinking of the resources available to you, in the same way that your sales and marketing team think about reaching potential customers. You need to not just capture your employees' attention with a union-free operating philosophy, but you must hold it and continue to communicate that philosophy with them until you've created a genuinely union-proof culture.

Let's get started with a nine-step proactive strategy, the first step of which should be reviewing your company's hiring and selection process. Dig deep into how your human resources team finds like-minded candidates who are both a fit for the position and the organization as a whole, including the company's union-free philosophy. Your union-proof hiring process needs to include the following:

- Background checks
- Multiple interviews for each prospective new hire
- Reference checks: remember the tactic of "salting" by organizers!

Also, your interviewers should understand the legal "do's and don'ts" of the job interview process, including what they can ask candidates. There are a lot of resources online for some good, basic interviewing guidelines.

A well-trained interviewer speaks volumes about the company and the respect they have for the potential new hire. Demonstrating that, even before someone is hired, sets a professional tone for your organization and creates an understanding of how your union-free culture benefits everyone.

The next part of your proactive strategy should be to address your company's wage and benefits structure. Now, this may not be something you have direct control over, but you should conduct regular research to make sure that what you're offering is competitive in your industry and your marketplace. Trust me, if you aren't doing this research, the unions are, and they have no problem with presenting it to your employees. A genuinely union-proof company differentiates itself from unionized workers and industry competitors by providing competitive wage and benefit structures. These items should be reviewed and adjusted on an annual basis—or as needed.

Don't be afraid to get creative with your compensation! There are plenty of ways to develop unique compensation structures that will serve both the employees and the company equally well. One of the best ways to address this area is to ask employees for their input concerning wages, benefits, and other "perks" that might provide added value to their total compensation package. Sometimes just being included in the conversation via an employee survey can be enough to engage employees and prevent them from feeling like they need a union to be heard.

The next goal in your nine-step strategic approach to union-proofing should be centered around employee retention. Consider producing a "pre-hire" orientation video to provide job candidates with a solid understanding of not only the position but also of your company's culture—before they're ever offered the job. Retention rates are also improved when you make sure that every new hire is provided with a robust onboarding process. This process should include consistent messaging on your operating philosophy, direct connection between employees and management, and the ways in which employee concerns are addressed. Regular employee surveys and feedback can improve retention rates, so incorporate a periodic and consistent method for assessing employee engagement and satisfaction. Finally, reducing turnover can also come through an understanding of *why* employees leave. Make sure your human resources team engages in exit interviews. The knowledge gained from these can provide a tremendous opportunity to get ahead of workplace problems and keep your organization secure.

In your effort to protect workers from harassment, and to remain union-free, the fourth element in your preventive strategy should involve your union avoidance training. Begin by training your managers, and remember that union avoidance training isn't a "one-and-done" proposition. You should establish a plan for continuing education for the coming twelve months—at which point you'll want to revisit your plan, adjust for your specific needs, and create another year of training plans. It pays to get as comprehensive as possible with your union avoidance training: The better armed supervisors are, the better they'll be able to defend the next group that needs union avoidance education… your employees!

Now, you'll be the best judge of what's appropriate for your company's culture and your employees but begin union avoidance education as soon as possible with any new employees by sharing your pro-employee, union-free philosophy in an orientation message. Then you'll want to continue educating employees on a regular basis, on things such as the National Labor Relations Act, the cost of unionization, and perhaps what the phrase "right to work" means. Delivering consistent education is easy when you take advantage of available video and online resources. Once you've determined which messages you'd like to deliver, create a schedule for your union avoidance training. Your training campaign can include a combination of in-person meetings, video presentations, and e-Learning. This multimedia approach is highly effective, reaching every supervisor and every employee on a regular basis.

Step five of your proactive strategy is the company's plan to involve your first line supervision. Your first line team can make a huge difference in your union-proofing efforts. To your employees, their first line supervisors *are* the company, which makes your managers the key to employee engagement.

This element of your strategy requires training and knowledge for your supervisors. One of the easiest ways to provide that insight is online training or eLearning. Supervisor training is a powerful foundation for your managers, providing them with the confidence they need to address employee concerns both legally and actually. Also, you might want to consider interactive eLearning programs on TIPS and FOE that will help your management team turn their knowledge into action.

Your nine-step proactive strategy should next include a focused effort on management visibility and accessibility. Make sure your managers are well-trained in positive employee relations, with knowledge in connecting, improving, supporting, and motivating your employees. You can do this by first explaining to your managers that their unique position in the company requires them to walk a fine line between engaging with their team members and being a company advocate. The confidence to be visible and accessible comes from regular training and reinforcement on topics such as morale-building, praise and recognition, and involving employees in decision-making.

Make it a priority that these interactions are perceived by employees as genuine and sustained, which can be achieved by having managers maintain an active presence on all shifts. Remember to train your supervisors and managers to walk through all work areas regularly and be available to their team members. Finally, make sure that your managers understand that team members value their presence, their attention, and feeling like they are a part of their management's commitment to the company culture.

And that leads us to the next important element of your proactive strategy, communication. Your managers and supervisors need more than just knowledge; they need a direct line to upper management that allows them to feel supported. One excellent way to achieve this is with an online resource such as a

LaborLook.com website, dedicated to labor relations and available at all times. (Tip: this is a Projections, Inc. product line.) On your manager-focused LaborLook.com site, include information about the union or unions most likely to attempt to organize your employees. Provide information about the company and your union-free operating philosophy, and perhaps most important of all, include a direct line of contact to upper management to report any possible organizing activity. Providing a method for two-way communication between managers and your employee relations team is key to being aware of any organizing activity early on. In many ways, your managers serve the same roles that unions claim to provide—advocacy, support, and representation to senior management. If managers aren't present to fill those roles, employees might just look to a union to do it for them. Today's labor climate dictates that the quicker your management team can address any employee concerns, the better chance you have at remaining union-free.

Your internal training campaign means that excellent communication needs to extend to your employees, as well. You should communicate with your employees consistently and as openly as is practical, on all matters affecting the business, human resources, labor relations, and the community. Care should be taken never to let the rumor mill replace corporate communication. An excellent way to get ahead of the early phases of an organizing drive—and to communicate regularly if a drive does take hold—is through a UnionFree.com website. (Tip: this is a Projections, Inc. product line.) This employee-focused tool can serve as an educational tool, an interactive communication platform, and a trusted factual resource.

And here's a strategy that many companies miss! Involve your employees' families in your communications. As important as it is to spread the good news or even the not-so-good news about the company with your employees, it's just as important to make sure that this information is shared with the people who influence your employees the most outside of work.

Step seven is to add your employee relations team to your proactive strategy. You want to build a "core team" of specially trained union-avoidance front-line supervisors as part of your employee relations team. This group of "first responders" can help your company to recognize any organizing activity early on, and help to keep upper management informed of any changes they observe in the workforce. Your "core team" can be used as a sounding board for policy changes, serve as communications liaisons between upper management and workers, and help to educate employees about the truth behind union promises. And maybe most importantly, this group can help train other front-line supervisors about unions and organizing as the need arises.

To create your "core team," you can either ask for volunteers or have upper management hand-select those most likely to excel in this type of role. Either way, focus on good "coverage," so that you have a "core team" member available at as many shifts and in as many locations as possible. Make sure your "core team" receives top-notch union avoidance training and is fully prepared to alert you when changes in employee sentiment are detected.

The eighth element of your nine-step proactive strategy is to review your handbook, your policies, and your procedures to ensure that the language used doesn't "chill" the Section 7 rights of your employees under the NLRA. To do this, first create clear policies for solicitation and distribution, the use of e-mail, and social media presence. Before you share those policies with your employees, be sure you have your labor attorney first review what you've written. And finally, make sure that your employee relations team knows the policies inside and out, that they aren't prone to overreact to possible policy violations, and that instead, they will be prepared to review any situation on its unique characteristics.

Finally, your proactive strategy must include a plan for employee involvement. This element of your preventive measures is highly valued by employees—and it's also something that can completely cancel out the need for a union in your employees' eyes. Often getting employees involved is easier said than done. But one of the easiest ways to get there is to look for opportunities to establish employee teams to provide and manage feedback, input, and suggestions. Employee teams will become a valuable extension of your employee relations team, and they can facilitate resolutions and positive morale throughout the organization. Other opportunities for employee involvement might include skip-level meetings, employee recognition, and corporate participation in community events, all of which empower employees and reinforce the idea that their voice is valued by your company—with no need for a third-party.

What all of this comes down to is the fact is that what's good for your employees can also be excellent for your union-avoidance efforts. By keeping your workplace positive, collaborative, and connected, you will strengthen the bonds between workers and management, building a "family" that works together to find solutions to their problems. What's more, when your team works together that well, it makes for a stronger company overall, one that can better serve your customers and meet your goals—which all adds up to a pretty good side benefit to becoming union-proof!

Your Union-Free Philosophy

Do you know whether your company has a written-out union-free philosophy? To be union-proof, you've got to communicate—from the top down—what exactly your operational objectives are with respect to unionization, and exactly what the company is willing to do to accomplish those goals. Without this core foundation, communicated clearly and consistently, it's impossible for individual employees and team members to define their roles in maintaining a union-proof culture.

I've talked about ways to keep unions at bay by being proactive, by demonstrating best practices as an employer, and by making your workplace so responsive to your employees that they won't ever feel the need for union representation. But to be truly union-proof, employees not only need to feel that they don't need a union, but they need to have ownership of the idea that unions wouldn't be right for the way they work. They need to understand that unions wouldn't line up with the company's corporate culture and that unions wouldn't serve the needs of their customers, their families, or their community. That's where your union-free philosophy statement comes in.

In the twenty-first century, it's not enough for a company to tell its workers to "Just Say No" to unions. Your employees are smart, media-savvy content consumers. Google has been at their fingertips, in some cases since their birth, and they need to be respected with a candid explanation of where the company stands on unionization. It needs to be something beyond a simple "Vote No." Your company may already have a union-free philosophy in place. If so, it is the foundation of your corporate labor-relations strategy, usually drafted by management at the highest organizational level.

Written correctly and reviewed by appropriate legal counsel, your union-free philosophy statement will help *protect* your company, not place you in a defensive position. Remember the T.I.P.S. and F.O.E. rules? The company is expressing an opinion that unionization isn't the right choice. In fact, your written statement can even clearly outline your employees' right to organize under the NLRA. Written and distributed correctly, a union-free philosophy statement can quickly become one of the most powerful tools in your union-proofing strategy.

First, let's talk about *corporate philosophies* in general. A *corporate philosophy* is any statement that defines the core beliefs that people in the company hold and by which they are guided. It works hand in hand with the company's mission, values, and vision statements, and along with the company's code of ethics, these statements help to define the company. Corporate philosophies are bold in their nature, and they set the tone for the company's culture, the way a company carries itself, and the things it considers to be important.

It's *important* to note here that a corporate philosophy is *not* the same thing as a *union-free* philosophy. Union-free philosophies are a *type* of corporate philosophy, focused strictly on the topic of labor relations and third-party representation. But as different as they are, both types of philosophies help to define a company, they both demonstrate a clear point of view, and in their own ways, they both share the same basic role: to inform the world of what the company is and what its goals are.

Your company's union-free philosophy should be a genuine statement, clearly explaining the company's belief in a union-free work environment. It may go into detailed reasons behind that thinking, or it may not. It may include language that acknowledges employees' Section 7 rights, or it might not. For companies with a small percentage of unionized workers, it might even mention that while they're committed to good-faith bargaining wherever they have unions, they still *prefer* a union-free working environment. Here are some ideas of what you'll want to include in *your* union-free philosophy.

First, make sure your statement explains the benefits of a workplace that is union-free so that your new employees understand the reasons behind it. Don't expect new hires to understand and embrace this way of thinking immediately —it may be new to them! But help them to understand how it serves every employee, and let them know that they can expect to grow from the way the company operates.

Then, express pride in the organization and what the team accomplishes together, and attribute that pride to the direct connection between management and employees. Mention your open-door policy, that employees are welcome to express concerns, issues, and ideas and that management will listen. If you have an alternative dispute resolution process in place, mention it, as well. Remind employees that a union-free environment encourages excellent two-way conversation!

Finally, reiterate the financial reasons behind your philosophy and how operating union-free provides greater opportunities for the company, its employees, their families, and the communities in which they live and work.

Bottom line: What your company chooses to include in your union-free philosophy statement is entirely up to your team, but it should be noted that most modern philosophies are less "anti-union" and more "pro-employee" in their approach.

As a rule, your statement should be written carefully, to confirm an accurate communication of your message, but also to keep the company on the right side of the law. To this end, you should consult legal counsel before publishing your union-free philosophy, to ensure that the wording doesn't violate any provisions of the NLRA.

Also, your statement shouldn't be considered timeless or ironclad—it should be reviewed on a regular basis to ensure its relevance in light of changing labor laws and labor environments.

This is particularly the case if you include your union-free philosophy statement in your employee handbook. As I discussed, the NLRB has issued statements, putting all employers on notice. The Board, when given the opportunity to investigate ULP charges, will aggressively scrutinize employee handbooks and policies for language that could have a "chilling effect" on exercising the right to engage in "protected concerted activity" under Section 7 of the NLRA. This direct or perceived violation of the NLRA is what a union organizer will use as proof to your employees of why a union is needed at your company. The writing of a union-free philosophy is critical, but the communication of that statement is just as important. Your company may have written the most stirring union-free philosophy ever drafted, but if no one reads it, what's the point?

Take some time out to create a communications strategy for releasing your philosophy, and make sure that the people who need to receive this message get it, loud and clear. Who are those people?

We'll start off with the earliest possible candidates: *new hire—and even pre-hire—employees.* Inform your new employees about your company's stance on unions from day one, by including your union-free philosophy in your orientation and pre-hire programs and materials. Your willingness to be open on this topic from the very beginning provides consistency, demonstrates the company's trustworthiness, and provides a foundation for respect in the company's beliefs. Communicating it from the beginning helps you stay true to your word, should a union campaign begin sometime down the road.

Once a union-free philosophy is established, many companies take the opportunity to go one step beyond the philosophy itself and include discussion and education on union authorization cards and what they mean. The truth is, at companies that haven't taken the time to build a union-proof culture, employees often sign union authorization cards without a second thought, not even considering that the company would prefer to operate union-free.

You'll also need to communicate this philosophy with your *current employees*. Even if your company hasn't changed their philosophy in years, current employees need a regular reminder of the company's thoughts on unionization—so reissue your employee handbook with your union-free philosophy prominently placed to keep everyone on the same page. Depending on your company culture, you may wish to put this statement on your company's intranet or employee portal, to keep it top of mind for all employees.

Now, let's talk about why—and how—you might want to consider sharing this union-free philosophy with *people outside of the organization*, such as customers and potential future business partners. A company that is union-free is a company free from the risk of a strike, free from the red tape of union contracts, and free to go the extra mile to meet its customers' needs. Depending on your industry and your operations, even placing your union-free philosophy on your company's public website or in agreements with vendors sends a message that your customers can count on your company without worrying about the negative impact of a third-party involvement.

A well-written, well-communicated union-free philosophy statement is a vital step in establishing your union-proof culture. It serves as an open, honest foundation for all future union-avoidance efforts, and it sets the tone for what employees and customers can expect from the company, regarding labor relations. Your union-free philosophy statement is not something to fear or to keep hidden, but rather to embrace! It works in tandem with your mission and vision statement, your corporate principles, core values, and your compliance and code of ethics. I encourage you to either review the union-free philosophy your company has in place or work with your executive team to develop one if it's yet to be established. It's a vital part of the foundation of your union-proof culture!

Defining Your Union-Free Culture

We have come a long way in "Proof Positive"! We started with an understanding of why you needed to become union-proof, and then we built from there with an inside look at how unions operate and how they organize. I shared with you the basics of what life is like with union. I've discussed how to become union-proof and how to communicate at all levels of your organization, and, well, that's why we're here, right? It's all about getting the entire company on board to create an environment where unions just aren't necessary!

It's about building that amazing culture, building a relationship between the people in your organization, and influencing them to take ownership of their own union-free future.

This book came about when I discovered that companies that were once afraid to fight back against unions were open to the new realities of staying union-free; they just didn't know how to do it. So, our team began teaching them everything—from how corruption has influenced union operations, to the truth about how much a strike can cost employees. We gave them the knowledge we had gained from almost four decades in helping companies stay union-free.

And now *you* have that knowledge, as well. Which means it's time for *you* to get started!

There's no luck involved here, and union-proofing by hoping the unions never come calling is pretty useless, and I've seen a lot of "unionized" companies go this route. But start the conversation—start asking your managers and employees to respond to you, conduct a vulnerability assessment and ask them to tell you what their biggest concerns are, what their biggest dreams are, what their biggest hopes are, what's keeping them awake at night—start that conversation!

I'm talking an actual strategy, a hands-on, roll-up-your-sleeves, step-by-step plan to keep your company union-free. And now you're ready to do the work that "Proof Positive" has been preparing you for—and that's to become a trusted educator. Your employees probably don't have the luxury of learning about unions in a classroom environment. So, to create a union-proof legacy, it will be up to you to educate them, by making conversations about labor unions a regular part of your workplace discussions.

About what kinds of things can you talk? Training your workforce on unions can start as effortlessly as discussing current affairs—when a unionized plant in your town goes out of business, for example, or when a national strike shuts down an airline, a supplier, or even a professional sports team. Anything to get the conversation going—because not only do these conversations pass along valuable information to your employees, but they frame you as someone who is knowledgeable about unions. That makes you a trusted and valued resource in their eyes, which is very helpful, especially if a union begins a campaign among your employees.

Now, this is an important point, and I want to you to pause here to reflect for a moment. When your employees begin to see *you* as that valuable resource, as someone who is knowledgeable about unions, *own it*, because *you've earned it!*

Before I get started outlining your educational strategy, I want to point out that you've got great tools available to you. Many companies don't have that when they begin working on being union-free. They have bits and pieces of what they need, but not a full understanding of the tools and methods that are required. This gives you a huge advantage in becoming an employer-of-choice and becoming truly union-proof.

As I have discussed, before you even begin crafting your strategy, the very first thing to do is to establish your union-free philosophy statement, which you should have accomplished at this point.

With that written, you now need to begin communicating it with your current employees. Creating a video that teaches your philosophy and connects with your employees will provide that clear, consistent voice your team needs. This kind of message builds trust and understanding.

For new hires, you'll want to create a similar type of communication. Some companies choose to produce a short "pre-hire orientation" message that is delivered to candidates even before they are offered a job. This approach ensures that your philosophy is understood from the start.

Once a new-hire candidate accepts the position, then you can communicate additional information in your orientation message, including why a third party wouldn't benefit the company, its employees, or its customers. You might even want to begin the education process on card signing at this time.

Can you see how providing every employee with this clear, consistent messaging can make a world of difference in your union-proofing goals? Every employee can share in this joint, "tribal" knowledge.

Now, what about managers and supervisors? Where do they figure into your strategy? Ask any labor-relations expert and they'll quickly tell you: Organizing campaigns are often won or lost based on the strength of your front-line management.

Here's where taking advantage of the tools available to you can really be an asset. Start by providing necessary labor-relations training, so that your managers have the confidence to observe their employees and understand their roles. At that point, they can be prepared to turn their knowledge into action. Creating great leaders is a huge part of staying union-free. Your company leaders need a whole host of skills that aren't specific to unions. They need to learn how to support, improve, motivate, and connect with your employees. When employees are engaged and happy, they won't feel the need to seek out a union. And if the union comes to your company on its own, satisfied employees are much less likely to be manipulated into signing a union authorization card.

Toward this end, companies should provide ongoing, regular education and opportunities for conversations with employees. This can include education on card signing, the cost of unionization, what "right to work" really means, their rights under the National Labor Relations Act, or any of a host of other topics.

In the next part of your strategy, consider whether or not an alternative dispute resolution process would be right for your company and your union-proofing culture. This is something that's particular to each company, but when coupled with transparency and consistent communication, it can represent a huge leap forward in eliminating the need for a union.

Once you've laid the foundation for ongoing communications, you may want to consider building a custom website just for your managers. Typically, this site should include interactive training, union-specific information, access to your company's union-free philosophy, and even resources that allow managers to report observations of possible organizing activity.

Creating a site dedicated to remaining union-free that is specifically for managers demonstrates that the union-proof culture is real, as you're providing your management with the tools and knowledge they need to feel confident and supported as they promote a union-proof culture in the workplace.

You may also want to create a website for employees—but you might keep this in your back pocket...what you might call "in the dark," or better yet, call it your "Ready-Set-Go" strategy. Should a unionization campaign begin, you will be ready to communicate clearly, consistently, openly, and honestly with your employees!

Now, sometimes you can build a great strategy, including everything I've mentioned here, and still end up being the target of a union campaign. It happens, and frankly, some companies—particularly successful ones with lots of employees and therefore a high potential for union dues income—can become too tempting of a target for a union to ignore. Clearly, the presence of a union campaign in your workplace isn't an indictment of your company's union-proof status, not by a long shot. Just because a union is attempting to influence your employees, that doesn't automatically mean they're about to start collecting dues. In fact, all the presence of a union campaign means to a union-proof company is that your union-proof plan is about to kick into high gear!

If you become aware of an organizing or card-signing union campaign at your company, your union-proof strategy should immediately begin with your labor-relations team, even if the team is just you. Start by enlisting the resources you previously developed. Contact your labor attorney; reach out to your consultants. Get online and send a message to employee communication providers for additional content such as videos, websites, and eLearning resources.

One thing to note here: If you conducted a vulnerability study early on in your union-proofing strategy—and if you continued to survey your employees, doing so now is just a matter of course. But if you're concerned about what employees are thinking, and you conduct a survey for the first time after a union campaign begins, you are putting your company at the very real risk of an Unfair Labor Practice charge. Stay connected to your employees by regularly asking them for their feedback before a union campaign ever begins.

As a union-proof company, you've already established much of what you'll need to stay union-free. Your labor-focused website for managers can continue to be a trusted source for the most up-to-date information on the campaign. And again, if you've included a website for employees in your strategy, you've got an instant resource with which to begin an open dialogue regarding the union's claims and promises. If a union gets enough cards signed to petition for an election, your strategy should be to educate employees on how unions organize, on their job security, on collective bargaining, and also on strikes!

Be sure to include a final meeting that includes a 25th Hour presentation the day before a vote. This clear and consistent message reminds employees of all the information they've received to date, and it shares the company's hopes on how the vote will be resolved.

Remember that if you want to stay union-free, you've got to work to become union-proof! It's not enough anymore to just respond to a union threat; you've got to plan for it, far in advance, and proactively make that plan part of your corporate culture.

So, there is your union-proof strategy, but it's not the end of your education! Your company's union-proof efforts must continue to grow and evolve. Union tactics are constantly changing, as are the legal guidelines under which we all must operate. Union-proof companies like yours must keep current to stay ahead of the unions. What's important here is that you simply get started.

Your union-proof legacy starts now!

ADVERTISEMENT

Get What You Need to Create a Union-Proof Culture
Union-Proof Certification
Is Now Available!

Labor Relations Has Changed...

Once upon a time, staying union-free was reactionary and defensive. It involved a lot of negativity. Companies relied on heavy-handed tactics to keep organizers from gaining a foothold. And as long as the company offered a decent living wage, they intentionally avoided the need to even say the word *union*, lest they plant ideas in the heads of their workers.

Those days are long gone.

Today, businesses are forced to navigate new rules, laws, and regulations every year, just to keep ahead of labor requirements, and needless to say...they can't do it alone.

That's where YOU come in...

Today, companies need skilled labor relations professionals who can:

- Leverage knowledge of the culture of organized labor to predict what they might do next.
- Architect proactive campaign strategies that can be called upon to address labor issues.
- Understand how unions operate: their finances, their constitutions, and what those standard operating procedures can do to the company.
- Build and grow company advocates...without resorting to unethical tactics.
- Stay on top of the latest developments in labor relations in order to know how—and when—to react.

ADVERTISEMENT

- Track and measure the vulnerability risk of unionization on an ongoing basis.
- Establish an *employees-first* labor communications strategy that enhances the employer's brand and helps to recruit and retain the best talent.

By the end of this class, you'll possess all of these skills, and so much more...

INTRODUCING UNION-PROOF CERTIFICATION
Become the most trusted labor-relations professional in the room by mastering the six critical core disciplines of union-proofing...

Then, bring these skills together and become a *Certified Union-Proof Professional*!

ADVERTISEMENT

HOW IT WORKS

Each unit is designed to be completed in a week (although students are allowed to work at their own pace).

On Tuesdays...
...you'll receive access to the streaming video lessons for that particular class. Each class typically contains about ten to fifteen minutes of video, as well as printable handouts and an activity that will help make the information relevant and applicable to your specific company and your unique situation.

On Fridays...
...you'll attend a twenty-minute office hours session, during which you can get your questions answered and receive help in completing your binder activities.

On Mondays...
...you'll take the session test and receive feedback on your answers. Once you complete all six units, you will then be eligible to take the exam for the coveted *Certified Union-Proof Professional* designation.

COURSE BREAKDOWN

Each week, for twenty-four weeks, you will master a new union-proofing topic. Along the way, you'll complete homework, be provided with instructor feedback, and receive certifications after successful completion of each unit exam. Here's how each week is broken down:

ADVERTISEMENT

UNIT 1
WEEKS 1 AND 2
THE HISTORY OF UNIONS

Before you can understand the culture of organized labor, you've got to understand how that culture developed. Who are the unions, where did they come from, and how do their origins affect how they operate today? In this opening unit, we'll answer all of these questions, as well as outline the union-proof journey so you can clearly articulate the role your team plays in it. We'll also determine which unions you should focus your energy on, so you can deploy a *focused* communications strategy the right way, the first time.

UNIT 2
WEEKS 3 AND 4
WHY BECOME UNION-PROOF?

Most businesses have some understanding of the challenges unionization can bring, but very few have insight into how intentionally remaining union-free can positively impact their company. That's where you come in. In these sessions, you'll gain specific tools to help your company focus on becoming union-proof while simultaneously reducing the overall risk of third-party involvement in the business.

UNIT 3
WEEKS 5 THROUGH 8
ORGANIZED LABOR: AN INSIDE LOOK

Intimate knowledge of how organized labor operates isn't an "optional extra" to be gained on the fly... It's an essential aspect of any labor-relations professional's ability to create a truly union-proof company. In this unit, you'll gain our exclusive insights into the nature of the business of unions, including a deep dive into

ADVERTISEMENT

their finances and constitutions, and a discussion on how easy it is for union leaders to become corrupt. Plus, you'll gain an insider's perspective on the National Labor Relations Board.

UNIT 4
WEEKS 9 THROUGH 15
ORGANIZING

Companies today must have strategic plans that address the very real possibility of organizing activity if they truly want to create a union-proof culture. In this unit, you'll learn the three ways a union can make inroads into a company. Plus, you'll gain the skills you need to help the company recognize organizing (even in its subtlest forms), take action through excellent communication, and avoid even the possibility of legal issues...without breaking the bank.

UNIT 5
WEEKS 16 THROUGH 18
LIFE WITH A UNION

Staying union-free is optimal, but sometimes challenges do lead to unionization. In this unit, you'll gain a solid foundation and understanding of the unique nature of a unionized workforce. You'll learn what really happens at the bargaining table and gain an understanding of the ways in which managing in a union environment can challenge your company's culture. By the time you finish this unit, you'll be able to effectively answer questions about what unionization is like, while simultaneously avoiding it at your company.

UNIT 6
WEEKS 19 THROUGH 24
GETTING UNION-PROOF

Thanks to an ever-changing political landscape, organized labor has successfully altered the way workers receive information on

ADVERTISEMENT

unionization, and most importantly, limited the way companies are able to communicate on this topic. Union-proof companies must learn to adapt to these changes and put relevant plans in place to educate, engage, and listen to employees. In this unit, you'll learn the importance of assessing your company's vulnerability to organizing, and how to set the expectations for a union-proof culture that will resonate throughout the company. You'll also gain practical proactive and preventive tools that work *today* and will continue to work *tomorrow*.

SHOULD YOU TAKE THIS COURSE?
It depends…

- **If you are a labor-relations professional** looking to gain an edge in an increasingly crowded marketplace…then yes.
- **If you are a traditional human resources professional** looking to get up-to-speed on labor relations…then yes.
- **If you are the leader of a human resources or labor relations team,** looking for strategies to build a union-proof culture without spending a fortune…then yes.
- **If you are a business owner** looking to stay union-free for the long-term…then yes.
- **If you are a crazy-busy C-suite executive or business owner** who barely has time to answer your e-mail…then *no!* (But you *should* have someone on your team become certified, because surrounding yourself with people smarter than you makes you smarter than everyone!)

**LET US
HELP YOU
BECOME THE MOST TRUSTED LABOR-RELATIONS
PROFESSIONAL IN THE ROOM!**

Visit http://unionproof.com/certification
for more information and to apply for our next class.

BIBLIOGRAPHY

Hoffa, James P. "Teamsters put corruption in its past" *http://www.usatoday.com/story/opinion/2015/01/14/teamsters-consent-decree-james-hoffa/21750913/ USA Today.* 14 Jan. 2015. Web. 05 Oct. 2015.

Goldwater, Barry. "Barry Goldwater, The Conscience Of A Conservative." *http://www.freerepublic.com/focus/news/1205133/posts Free Republic. Personal Archives | 1960 Barry Goldwater.* 01 Sept. 2004. Web. 10 Nov. 2015

Nygarrd, Richard Lowell. "Caterpillar v. International Union, United Automobile Workers of America" http://www.leagle.com/decision/19971159107F3d1052_11013/CATERPILLAR%20v.%20INTERNATIONAL%20UNION,%20UNITED%20AUTO.%20WORKERS%20OF%20AMERICA *Leagle.com.* 04 Mar. 1997. Web. 14 Dec. 2015

Troy, Leo. The Finances of American Unions, 1962-1969." http://www.nber.org/chapters/c7410.pdf *National Bureau of Economic Research. Exploration in Economic Research, Volume 2, Number 2.* 1975. Web. 15 Oct. 2015

Hagenbaugh, Barbara. "USATODAY.com – U.S. manufacturing jobs fading away fast." http://usatoday30.usatoday.com/money/economy/2002-12-12-manufacture_x.htm *USA Today.* 12 Dec. 2002. Web. 24 Mar. 2016

Kersey, Paul. "Executive Summary" http://www.mackinac.org/9964 *Mackinac Center*. 28 Aug. 2008. Web. 04 Apr. 2016

"Union Facts | Use of Dues for Politics." https://www.unionfacts.com/article/political-money/ *Unionfacts.com*. Web. 30 Oct. 2015

Mix, Mark. "Big Labor, big spender" http://www.usatoday.com/story/opinion/2013/09/02/labor-unions-politics-column/2731185/ *USA Today*. Web. 09 Oct. 2015

Noyes, Matt. "Whose "IBEW" is it? An Electrician online." https://www.uniondemocracy.org/UDR/113-Whose%20IBEW%20is%20it%20—%20an%20Electrician%20online.htm *Union Democracy Review*. 01 Feb. 2006. Web. 04 Nov. 2015

List, Peter "1-888-NO-UNION.COM." http://www.1-888-no-union.com/ibewconstitution.html Web. 28 Mar. 2016

Alston, Jr., Rossie D. and Taubman, Glenn M. "Union Discipline and Employee Rights" http://www.nrtw.org/RDA.htm *National Right to Work | Legal Defense Foundation, Inc.*, Web. 30 Dec. 2015

DeBare, Ilana. "Teamster Fine UPS Worker / San Jose man must pay $10,000 for denouncing strike on TV" http://www.sfgate.com/business/article/Teamsters-Fine-UPS-Worker-San-Jose-man-must-pay-3012510.php *SFGATE*. 26 Feb. 1998. Web. 07 Oct. 2015

Wilkerson, Matt. "If employer commits ULPs and win the election the NLRB may…" https://www.coursehero.com/file/p1dgag/If-employer-commits-

ULPs-and-win-the-election-the-NLRB-may-invalidate-the/ *Boise State | Business Law.* 2010. Web. 24 Nov. 2015

"Interfering with employee rights (Section 7 & 8(a)(1)" https://www.nlrb.gov/rights-we-protect/whats-law/employers/interfering-employee-rights-section-7-8a1 *NLRB.* Web. 07 Mar. 2016

Freeman, Matthew D., Rosen, Philip B., Bloom, Howard M., Greenberg, Richard I., Schudroff, Daniel D. "NLRB General Counsel Issues Guidance to Employers on 'Chilling Effects' of Personal Policies under National Labor Relations Act" http://www.jacksonlewis.com/resources-publication/nlrb-general-counsel-issues-guidance-employers-chilling-effects-personnel-policies-under-national-labor *Jackson Lewis.* 20 Mar. 2015. Web. 23 Dec. 2015.

O'Brien, Christine Neylon. "The Top Ten NLRB Cases on Facebook Firings and Employer Social Media Policies" http://www.alsb.org/wp-content/uploads/2013/11/NP-2013-OBrien_Top-Ten-NLRB.pdf *Forthcoming Oregon Law Review Volume 92 Issue 2.* 01 Jan. 2014. Web. 13 Nov. 2015.

"Is It Too Much To Ask For A Little Courtesy From Employees?" http://blog.rhoadssinon.com/is-it-too-much-to-ask-for-a-little-courtesy-from-employees/
Rhoads & Sinon LLP. Web. 22 July 2016

"The NLRB Shakes Things Up: Purple Communications and the Board's New 'Ambush' Elections Rule" http://www.natlawreview.com/article/nlrb-shakes-things-purple-communications-and-board-s-new-ambush-elections-rule *Neal, Gerber & Eisenberg, LLP.* 19 Dec. 2014. Web. 09 Nov. 2015.

Mayer, Gerald "Labor Union Certification Procedures: Use of Secret Ballots and Card Checks" http://congressionalresearch.com/RL32930/document.php *Congressional Research, prepared for Members and Committees of Congress*. Web. 17 Nov. 2015.

O'Keefe, Bryan M. "National Labor Relations Board Permits Employees to Use Workplace Email Systems for Union Activity" https://www.bakerlaw.com/alerts/national-labor-relations-board-permits-employees-to-use-workplace-email-systems-for-union-activity *Baker & Hostetler LLP*. 15 Dec. 2014. Web. 20 Oct. 2015.

Carter, Mark A. "NLRB Permits Micro-Units In Specialty Healthcare Decision" http://www.dinsmore.com/nlrb_permits_micro_units/ *Dinsmore & Shohl LLP*. 08 Sept. 2011. Web. 09 Nov. 2015.

"NLRB Deems Micro-Unit an Appropriate Bargaining Unit in Retail Industry" http://www.duanemorris.com/alerts/nlrb_deems_micro-unit_appropriate_bargaining_unit_retail_industry_5269.html *Duane Morris LLP*. 01 Aug. 2014. Web. 15 Nov. 2015.

Ramsey, Natalie K. "Beware the microunit: Court upholds NLRB's bargaining unit standard" http://www.mcafeetaft.com/beware-the-microunit-court-upholds-nlrbsbargainingunitstandard *McAfee & Taft*. 01 Dec. 2013. Web. 23 Nov. 2015.

Redmond, Sean P. "A Rose By Any Other Name is Still a Union" https://www.uschamber.com/article/rose-any-other-name-still-union *U.S. Chamber of Commerce*. 07 Aug. 2013. Web. 19 June 2016.

"Interfering with employee rights (Section 7 & 8(a)(1))" https://www.nlrb.gov/rights-we-protect/whats-law/employers/interfering-employee-rights-section-7-8a1 *NLRB*. Web. 04 Mar. 2016.

"Shaw's Supermarkets, Inc., Petitioner, v. National Labor Relations Board, Respondent, 884 F.2d 34 (1st Cir. 1989)" http://law.justia.com/cases/federal/appellate-courts/F2/884/34/463635/ *Justia US Law*. 31 Aug. 1989. Web. 01 May. 2016.

"Federal judge orders Chicago bus company to rehire drivers, stop interrogating employees" https://content.govdelivery.com/accounts/USNLRB/bulletins/3d5f59 *NLRB News Release*. 24 April. 2012. Web. 27 April. 2016.

"NLRB Judge finds recurring unlawful interference, orders third election at New York egg processing plant" https://www.nlrb.gov/news-outreach/news-story/regional-news-nlrb-judge-finds-recurring-unlawful-interference-orders-third *NLRB News Release*. 02 May. 2011. Web. 28 April. 2016.

Nelson, Krista. "Employee Use of Social Media and Email" https://www.stokeslaw.com/blog/stokes-law-briefs/post/employee-use-of-social-media-and-email *Stokes Lawrence*. 28 Mar. 2016. Web. 22 July. 2016.

Guerin, J.D., Lisa. "Unfair Labor Practices" http://www.nolo.com/legal-encyclopedia/unfair-labor-practices.html *NOLO*. Web. 02 May. 2016.

"Section 8(e) – Enforcement of a Lawful 'Hot Cargo' Clause Against a 'Neutral' Contractor" http://scholarship.law.upenn.edu/cgi/viewcontent.cgi?article=6176&context=penn_law_review *Penn Law | Legal Scholarship Repository*. Web. 01 May. 2016.

"Unfair Labor Practices" http://www.berrylegal.com/practices/Unfair_Labor_Practices/ *Berry & Berry PLLC.* Web. 24 Jan. 2016.

Owoseni, Omosolape Olakitan. "Collective Bargaining As A Veritable Tool For Resolving Conflicts in Organizations" http://www.wbiconpro.com/424-Omo.pdf *Ajayi Crowther University.* Web. 04 Nov. 2015

McKeever, Shaley "3 Types of Employees: How to Spot the Silent Killer." https://www.recruiter.com/i/3-types-of-employees-how-to-spot-the-silent-killer/ *Recruiter.com.* 31 Jan 2014. Web. 16 Nov. 2015

Crabtree, Steve "Can Managers Engage Union Employees?" http://www.gallup.com/businessjournal/22735/Can-Managers-Engage-Union-Employees.aspx *Gallup.* 11 May 2006. Web. 02 June 2016

"APA Survey Finds Feeling Valued at Work Linked to Well-Being and Performance." http://www.apa.org/news/press/releases/2012/03/well-being.aspx *American Psychological Association.* 8 Mar. 2012. Web. 14 June 2016

Joseph, Chris "The Advantages of A Unionized Workplace." http://smallbusiness.chron.com/advantages-unionized-workplace-15286.html *Small Business. Chron.* Web. 25 Mar. 2016

"Employee Strikes." http://www.referenceforbusiness.com/small/Di-Eq/Employee-Strikes.html *Advameg.* Web. 16 Oct. 2015

"DOL Issues Final Clarification of Persuader Rule." http://www.constructionequipment.com/dol-issues-final-clarification-persuader-rule *Mediapress Studios*. 25 Mar 2016. Web. 29 Mar. 2016

"Your Rights during Union Organizing" https://www.nlrb.gov/rights-we-protect/whats-law/employees/i-am-not-represented-union/your-rights-during-union-organizing *NLRB*. Web 28 Apr. 2016

Arnold, Michael. "Back At It Again: NLRB Invalidates Employer's Overbroad Solicitation Rule." https://www.employmentmattersblog.com/2014/12/back-at-it-again-nlrb-invalidates-employers-overbroad-solicitation-rule/ *Mintz Levin*. 15 Dec 2014. Web. 04 May 2016

Deitchler, Dale "Solicitation and Distribution Rules and Their Enforcement Under Attack: NLRB Continues to Narrow Employer Limitations on Workplace Communications" https://www.littler.com/solicitation-and-distribution-rules-and-their-enforcement-under-attack-nlrb-continues-narrow *Littler Mendelson P.C.* 11 Dec 2014. Web. 08 May 2016

"Make Sure Your No-Solicitation/No-Distribution Policy Does Not Violate the NLRA" http://www.shawe.com/publications/270-make-sure-your-no-solicitation-no-distribution-policy-does-not-violate-nlra *Shawe Rosenthal LLP.* 31 May 2013. Web 15 June 2016

Andrews, Walter J. and Levine, Michael S. "Top 10 Employment Liability Concerns" https://www.shrm.org/hr-today/news/hr-magazine/Pages/070815-employment-liability.aspx *SHRM*. 13 Jul 2015. Web. 27 Jul. 2016.

"Client Bulletins Can Your Employment Policies Survive the NLRB?" http://www.constangy.com/communications-500.html *Constangy, Brooks, Smith & Prophete, LLP.* 6 Feb 2014. Web. 08 Aug. 2016

CPSIA information can be obtained
at www.ICGtesting.com
Printed in the USA
FFHW02n0746290818
48136174-51841FF